ELEMENTS OF AGRICULTURAL TRADE POLICIES

Elements of Agricultural Trade Policies

James P. Houck

University of Minnesota

MACMILLAN PUBLISHING COMPANY
NEW YORK

Collier Macmillan Publishers
LONDON

Macmillan Publishing Company
866 Third Avenue, New York, NY 10022

Collier Macmillan Canada, Inc.

Printed in the United States of America

printing number   year

1 2 3 4 5 6 7 8 9 10   6 7 8 9 0 1 2 3 4 5

Library of Congress Cataloging-in-Publication Data

Houck, James P.
  Elements of agricultural trade policies.

  Bibliography: p.
  Includes index.
  1. Produce trade—Government policy. I. Title.
HD9000.6.H65 1986   382'.41   85-24211
ISBN 0-02-947720-4

To

George Brandow and Elmer Learn
Respected mentors and singular gents

No nation was ever ruined by trade.
Benjamin Franklin

Contents

PART TWO: Protection by Importers

      Administrative Trade Distortions**   **81**

      Voluntary Quotas   82
      Administrative Trade Distortions   83
      Summary   85
      Questions   85
      Additional Readings   86

9 **Import and Consumption Subsidies**   **87**

      Import Subsidy   88
      Direct Consumption Subsidy   89
      Welfare Effects   91
      Summary   92
      Questions   92
      Additional Readings   93

PART THREE: Protection by Exporters

       Subsidies, and Promotion**   **97**

       Export Expansion and Dumping   97
       Export Subsidies   98
       Welfare Analysis of Export Subsidies   102
       Production Subsidies and Exports   103
       Export Promotion   106
       Noncommercial Exports: Food Aid   107
       Summary   109
       Questions   110
       Additional Readings   110

11 **Market and Price Discrimination**   **112**

       Market Discrimination with a Fixed Supply   113
       Distribution of Revenue and Supply Response   115
       Summary   118
       Questions   118
       Additional Readings   119

12 **Export Taxes, Controls, and Embargoes**   **120**

       Export Taxes   120
       Export Controls and Embargoes   125
       Summary   129
       Questions   130
       Additional Readings   130

PART FOUR: Other Trade Policy Topics

Acknowledgments

About 18 years' worth of students in agricultural trade policy classes at the University of Minnesota have grappled with me and the topics covered in this book. These students and many other colleagues in the University's Department of Agricultural and Applied Economics and elsewhere have my sincere appreciation for penetrating comments and criticisms offered over the years. A special word of thanks is definitely in order to Maury E. Bredahl for many helpful comments and suggestions.

Some of the material in these pages is descended from two previously published, coauthored pieces of mine. My two collaborators, one on each paper, were James G. Kendrick of the University of Nebraska and Peter K. Pollak of the World Bank. They have my thanks, but carry no responsibility for the current shape of our earlier ideas.

I would be foolish not to recognize the outstanding contributions of my longtime secretary/colleague, Mary Strait. Her careful, professional work in preparing the manuscript is very much appreciated. Someday she might even teach me to spell "seperate" correctly.

Finally, I must acknowledge those who made it possible for me to spend the autumn of 1983 along the Oregon coast where, with the help of the Pacific Ocean and a host of seagulls, I fashioned the form and style of this book.

James P. Houck

ELEMENTS OF AGRICULTURAL TRADE POLICIES

Chapter 1

Introduction and Scope

With each passing year, the national economies of the world intertwine more closely than ever. This economic interdependence evolves because international trade expands more rapidly than the world's output of goods and services. The estimated volume of all goods and services produced in the world has almost quadrupled since 1953 (Table 1.1). However, total international trade volume has increased almost sixfold. Although this relationship is not true for every nation on the planet, it is very pervasive.

In 1953 the value of international trade for the world as a whole was about 13 percent of the value of all goods and services produced. In 1982 it had grown to an estimated 20 percent. Hence, for every $100 worth of output produced currently, about $20 worth finds its way across international borders.

As the role of international trade increases around the globe and for most individual countries, the economics of trade and trade policy grows increasingly relevant for people concerned about commercial affairs. This book is an introduction to the basic economics of trade and trade policy. Although the topics discussed here have rather general application, the book's specific focus is on agricultural trade policy. As we will discover, agricultural trade and trade policy occupy a special niche in the discussion and analysis of world economic issues. Moreover, trade in agricultural goods has evolved dramatically in the three decades since 1953 (Table 1.1).

Even though growth in both agricultural production and trade has been slower than that in nonagricultural sectors, the relative expansion in agricultural

1

Table 1.1 Development of World Production and Exports, Selected Years, 1953 to 1982 (1953=100)

Year	World commodity output (volume)		World exports (volume)	
	Total	Agricultural	Total	Agricultural
1953	100	100	100	100
1963	168	130	194	167
1973	302	166	448	245
1982	375	200	582	349

Source: General Agreement on Tariffs and Trade (GATT), *International Trade*, Geneva, Switzerland, various annual issues.

trade compared with farm output has been faster than the comparable relative expansion in nonagricultural sectors. Since 1953, each 1 percent increase in world output of all goods and services has been accompanied by an average increase in trade of 1.3 percent. For agriculture, each 1 percent increase in output has been accompanied by a 1.8 percent trade increase. Thus, agriculture's worldwide dependence on trade has been growing even faster than industry's. This phenomenon is occurring even though the unique impediments to agricultural trade erected over the years by national governments severely inhibit trade expansion.

The central goal of this book is to convey the basic economics of many widely used agricultural trade policy schemes in a clear, uncluttered, and consistent way. The book is written for individuals who already have some grasp of economic principles, but it is not a high-powered text in theory or quantitative analysis. It explains and analyzes numerous trade policy mechanisms, one at a time. Some, like tariffs and quotas, will be familiar to many readers. Others, like mixing regulations, market discrimination, and export subsidies, may be less widely known. Effects of various trade policies on domestic and international prices, consumption, production, trade, and government revenue are examined. Some ideas about the effects of individual trade policies on general economic welfare are presented, but they do not occupy a dominant position in the analyses. However, no special mathematical expertise or theoretical sophistication in economics is required.

Partial equilibrium demand and supply functions are employed throughout the text as the foundation stones of analysis and illustration. An exception is the general equilibrium approach adopted in Chap. 2 to highlight the concepts of comparative advantage and specialization. Two-dimensional diagrams are heavily used to develop the reasoning and the arguments. Many of these diagrams are simple, but some are modestly complex and interconnected. To keep these illustrations as uncluttered as possible, we have pursued economy in the labeling of various lines, functions, and points. The flow of the individual argument dictated the way in which each diagram is labeled and described. Strict or rigorous conventions were not pursued.

Partial equilibrium has its shortcomings. It short-circuits broad, economywide consideration of trade policy effects. However, partial equilibrium reasoning is relatively easy to grasp and provides an indispensable first step to understanding the operational vocabulary and major direct effects of various trade intervention schemes.

Because the emphasis is on economic principles and analysis, the presentation may seem somewhat abstract and stylized. Specific agricultural trade issues and problems of the day are not presented in their real-world detail. This is because the purpose of the book is to establish clearly the economic elements of individual trade policy schemes without reference to particular current controversies, countries, or commodities.

In the real world of international affairs, most trade policy schemes do not fit into single, unmistakable categories. Their inherent complexity diminishes their value as illustrative examples of specific types of policy. Numerous assumptions and qualifications would be needed to bend most real-world trade policy examples to the purpose of this book. Hence, our examples and illustrations are mainly hypothetical and generic. However, they are obviously drawn from typical trade policy questions faced by decision makers. The specific study questions posed at the end of each chapter are also largely hypothetical, yet they have clear parallels in today's farm and trade policy arena. The ideas they are meant to convey will be relevant not only this year and next year, but indefinitely.

The philosophical tone of this book is mostly neutral and nonjudgmental about trade barriers and government intervention in agricultural matters. Governments—past, present, and future—have intervened and will continue to intervene in agricultural trade. Our aim is not to argue for or against such intervention in principle but to examine the major economic effects of the intervention methods most frequently used. However, the consistent use of neoclassical economic theory surely provides a built-in bias toward market efficiency and laissez-faire. But that tendency is not exploited in a normative way in these pages.

To keep the number of topics manageable, the emphasis is on the individual nation rather than the global economy. Effects and implications of agricultural trade policy schemes are discussed largely from the immediate viewpoint of the nation enacting them. However, international impacts of various trade policies are not ignored. In addition, policy schemes are discussed and analyzed one at a time, as if they were established in isolation from each other and from broader economic and social changes. Their economic effects are generally compared with free trade results as if they were simple departures from free trade.

Naturally, this is not the way the real world operates. Economic life is in constant flux; individual trade policy schemes are often only building blocks of complex intervention systems; and free trade is rare indeed, especially in agriculture. But the objective of this book is not to exhaust the reality of international trade or to teach readers how to do it. Its modest aim is to explain and illuminate the economic elements and terminology of typical trade policies without the distracting influence of unnecessary detail. Because this is a book about basic economic analysis, it is not a source of facts or information about particular institutions, nations, or commodities. Free trade results are the norm for comparison, not because free trade is often a realistic alternative but because it is a consistent benchmark that can be employed across all types of intervention schemes.

This book does not pretend to be a fully rigorous treatment of the selected topics, nor is the selection of topics exhaustive. Most of the ideas and approaches are not wholly novel. They are now widely scattered throughout the literature of international trade and trade policy. A major contribution of this volume is to collect them together in a single, consistent presentation with agricultural trade applications at the forefront. The readings listed at the end of individual chapters are selected as additional references for the interested general reader rather than the research scholar.

After the Introduction, the 15 remaining chapters are grouped into four main sections. Part 1 presents in three chapters the general economic concepts underlying the theory of trade and its agricultural trade applications. Ideas about trade policy and protection as national objectives are introduced, along with a discussion about why and how agriculture is usually singled out for special economic treatment by trading nations. Then the partial equilibrium analytical foundation for virtually all the subsequent trade policy analyses is laid out.

Parts 2 and 3, with five and three chapters respectively, discuss various trade policy schemes pursued by importer and exporter nations. The mechanisms for protecting producers, consumers, or both from international competition are highlighted.

Part 4 contains four chapters dealing with some additional topics in trade policy economics. These include intermediate versus final goods in trade, trade preferences and economic integration, currency exchange rates, and overall trade stability in a protectionist world.

Part One

The Economic Setting

The craft of the merchant is this bringing a thing from where it abounds to where it is costly.

Ralph Waldo Emerson

Chapter 2

Basic Concepts: Comparative Advantage, Specialization, and Gains from Trade

This chapter describes the basic building blocks of international trade theory. It highlights some of the special characteristics of international exchange that once led a British statesman to write, "Free trade . . . is in almost every country unpopular." This remark, made about 150 years ago, could have been penned yesterday. As we discuss the basic concepts of trade, it is important to remember that trade theory, like all economic theory, is a simplification of reality. With it we can clarify and understand the fundamental forces at work even as governments, institutions, and problems change. Our purpose in this chapter is to give an overview of general equilibrium trade theory as a prelude to the pointed analyses of specific agricultural trade policies that follow in later chapters.

Trade can be examined from several viewpoints. One involves individual buyers and sellers; another involves particular commodity markets; still another is the viewpoint of a nation and its economic position relative to other nations. The classical development of trade theory stems from this latter vantage point, considering each nation as an economic unit. Agricultural production and trade need not be singled out for specific attention in general trade theory, but the distinction between agricultural and industrial production and exchange is often employed, as in this chapter, to illustrate the crucial ideas.

THE NATION AS AN ECONOMIC UNIT

Trade theory concerns economic relations among nations. To focus on forces that shape these relations, this theory treats each nation as if all economic decisions affecting trade are made either by a single rational authority or by many small buyers and sellers in keen competition with each other. This is a crucial simplification but one that is also employed frequently in other economic theory fields.

Using the nation as the economic unit defines away many real and puzzling problems. For instance, in basic trade theory the nation-unit usually is assumed to employ its resources fully. Also, resource adjustments are assumed to occur smoothly and completely in response to changing conditions. Advanced trade theory explores the consequences of changing these stringent assumptions. Naturally, the analytical complexity increases. Yet few would quarrel with these fundamental assertions:

1 Economic resources can usually be reallocated more easily within a nation than among nations.
2 Language, law, institutions, and customs are generally more unifom within a nation than among nations.
3 Political barriers exist for international transactions; they do not have counterparts in purely domestic commerce.

These conditions are strong enough to justify using individual nations as economic units for trade analysis. The reasoning and the theoretical results that emerge can seem abstract and remote from everyday experience. But because they are stylized and stark, they expose the basic economic forces at work in the trading world.

CAUSES OF FOREIGN TRADE

Individual traders generally use current prices and costs to form their decisions. They buy goods and services wherever they can obtain them most cheaply. Then they sell them to buyers offering the highest prices. This behavior is observed both within and across national borders. Hence, early economists used it as a guiding principle to explain international trade. Accordingly, a country exports whatever it can produce more cheaply than others, and it imports those items others can produce more cheaply. A country has an "absolute advantage" in the production of a good if its production costs are lower than other countries' at prevailing prices and exchange rates.

The principle of absolute advantage appeals to common sense. But as our view expands from single products or industries to whole nations, the least cost or absolute advantage principle begins to blur. What if a nation has an absolute advantage in all its products because of very cheap labor, abundant resources, or highly sophisticated technology? Although this is very unlikely, the logic of absolute advantage suggests that this nation would export products but import nothing. Why would a nation wish to do this? What would it do with its export earnings? These questions and others led economists to develop the idea of "comparative advantage."

The theory of comparative advantage was first stated clearly by David Ricardo in 1817. It has since been refined and extended by other economists. Instead of looking at the absolute costs of individual products, the comparative advantage idea suggests that we consider the cost of producing additional units of any one product in terms of the reduction necessary in the output of other goods. For example, to produce additional units of wheat, a nation would have to rearrange its resources, including perhaps land and labor. In doing so it might have to relinquish the opportunity to produce some units of corn or some automobiles.

The theory suggests that we compare these "opportunity" costs (e.g., the value of corn and cars given up) with comparable international prices. Then we should import goods for which the international price is less than the domestic opportunity cost of producing an additional unit at home. By the same logic, we should export products for which the international price is higher than the domestic opportunity cost of producing an additional unit. Resources released from producing imported goods can in principle be deployed in the production of export goods. Via specialization and trade, consumers in each trading nation can escape from the limited combinations of products available from only domestic resources. Through international exchange they can obtain a lower cost and a more abundant and wider selection of goods and services. Thus, in the context of comparative advantage, international trade rests on possible differences among countries in the rates at which production of one item can be replaced by another by means of internal resource adjustments. These differences in opportunity costs are the basis of comparative advantage, specialization, and mutually advantageous trade.

Mutually advantageous trade can arise among nations as long as these substitution rates differ. And they will differ where nations' climates, resources, people, and technologies differ. The principle of comparative advantage is symmetrical. That is, if a country has a comparative advantage in the production of one or more goods, then it must have a comparative disadvantage in the production of some other goods.

ILLUSTRATION OF SPECIALIZATION AND COMPARATIVE ADVANTAGE

Imagine two countries, Alphaland and Betaland. Each can use its resources and people to produce two major products—agricultural goods (F) and manufactured goods (M). Figure 2.1 shows Alphaland's possible outputs of F and M based on its particular combination of natural resources, capital, and people.

If Alphaland used all its resources in agriculture, it could generate 50 units

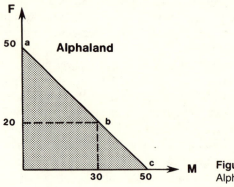

Figure 2.1 Production possibilities for Alphaland

of F per year and no units of M. This is point *a* in Fig. 2.1. If only manufactured goods were produced, 50 units of M could be had per year and no units of F (point *c*). By shifting resources between farms and factories, many output combinations of F and M are possible along the line *abc*. This line is called the "production" possibilities curve for Alphaland. Points inside *abc*, within the shaded area, are possible too. But they are inefficient, reflecting resource unemployment or underemployment. From any shaded-area point inside *abc*, more M or F (or both) can be obtained without sacrificing any output. However, along *abc*, more M can be obtained only at the expense of some F and vice-versa. The slope or steepness of *abc* reflects the rate at which F and M can be substituted for each other in production by rearranging fully used resources inside Alphaland. In this particular case, that rate of substitution is 1 F for 1 M. No output combination outside of *abc* is possible for Alphaland, given its resources.

If Alphaland is somehow isolated from exchange with Betaland or any other nation, then *abc* in Fig. 2.1 is also Alphaland's "consumption" possibilities curve. Without the prospect of international trade, a nation is restricted to consuming only the combinations of goods that it can produce itself. For instance, imagine Alphaland has organized its productive resources to produce 20 units of F and 30 units of M, at point *b* on its production possibilities curve. In isolation, Alphaland will be forced to limit its consumption choices to 20 F and 30 M. Any change in consumption will require an identical change in production along *abc*.

Now consider Betaland (Fig. 2.2). Notice that Betaland has a smaller economy than Alphaland. No matter what it does, Betaland cannot match the potential production of Alphaland in either F or M. Betaland could possibly produce 40 units of F (and no M) at point *d*, or 20 units of M (and no F) at point *j*. Any of the points along or inside Betaland's production possibilities curve *dej* are feasible, but only the points along *dej* are efficient. The rate at which F and M can be substituted for each other in production is different in Betaland than in Alphaland. For Betaland it is 2 units of F for 1 unit of M.

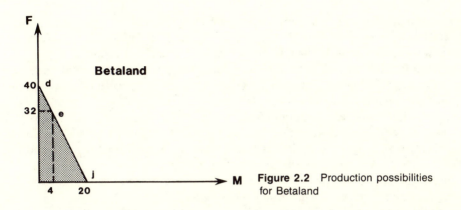

Figure 2.2 Production possibilities for Betaland

In isolation from trade, Betaland's consumption possibilities are confined to the area bounded by *dej*. If Betaland chooses to produce 32 units of F and 4 units of M at point *e*, it must consume that combination.

By opening up the possibility of international exchange between Alphaland and Betaland, we will see that both nations can break the link between national production and consumption. In doing so via trade, each country will be able to escape the confines of its own production possibilities curve and consume combinations of M and F that lie outside *abc* for Alphaland and *dej* for Betaland.

To visualize this process, first imagine that Alphaland is producing and consuming the combination of 20 F and 30 M denoted by point *b* in Fig. 2.1. Assume similarly that Betaland is at point *e* in Fig. 2.2, which is 32 F and 4 M. Now imagine taking Fig. 2.1 in your hand, flipping it over, and placing it upside down on Fig. 2.2 so that points *b* and *e* lie exactly on top of each other. This is point *e(b)* of Fig. 2.3. The size of the rectangle in Fig. 2.3 formed

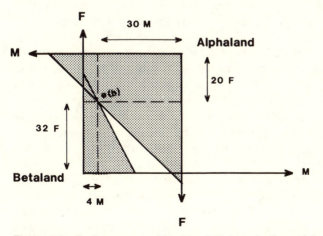

Figure 2.3 Trading opportunities from initial production points

by this maneuver is the total amount of F and M produced by Alphaland and Betaland together. This "world" output is 34 M and 52 F. Point *e(b)* shows how this world production is shared between the two. Betaland produces 4 units of manufactured goods and Alphaland contributes 30 units, the total being 34. On the other hand, Betaland produces 32 units of agricultural products while Alphaland grows 20 units, totaling 52.

Previously, these two nations were isolated from each other. Now suppose they look into possible international trades. Why might they wish to do this? For one thing, they could, via trade, separate the combination of F and M that each produces from the combination that each consumes. In Fig. 2.3 the two nations could possibly trade away from *e(b)* to *any* point inside the large rectangle by exchanging F and M with each other.

Alphaland would not be interested in any trade that would deliver it to a shaded-area point inside *abc* (Fig. 2.1). Those points are available to Alphaland without trade and are inefficient besides. Similarly, Betaland would disdain trades leading to shaded-area points inside *dej* (Fig. 2.2). However, there are points in the world production rectangle of Fig. 2.3 that are outside the capacity of each nation to achieve independently yet are available through trade. These are inside the unshaded area of Fig. 2.3. This unshaded area exists because the rate of substitution for F and M differs between Alphaland and Betaland. The greater the difference, the larger the unshaded area of potential exchange.

If these two nations are jointly producing F and M at point *e(b)*, demand and consumption analysis will show that in general the people of each nation can be better off if they trade away from *e(b)* down somewhere into the unshaded area. As we shall see, this potential for being better off is strengthened if we allow specialization to occur between the countries.

By allowing both exchange and production specialization to occur *simultaneously*, we see that trading nations always can make themselves better off. Consider Betaland again. Its original production and consumption position in isolation is point *e* in Fig. 2.4. Suppose that the international terms of exchange between F and M from Betaland's viewpoint are reflected by the slope of the line *egm*. That is, Betaland could continue to produce and consume at point *e*, or it could, without changing its production, export F and import M to any point along *egm*. Note that all points along *egm* lie outside Betaland's production possibilities curve. The line *egm* indicates the consumption possibilities of Betaland when trade is possible. As long as the terms of international exchange differ from the slope of the production possibilities curve, a trading nation can separate production and consumption combinations.

Imagine that Betaland found it advantageous to trade away from point *e* down to, say, point *g*, by exporting *ef* units of F and importing *fg* units of M. The selection of point *g* depends on the demand conditions in Betaland, but at least one such point will typically exist. Demand conditions are shaped by national income and its distribution, population, and the tastes and preferences of people. Consideration of this aspect of trade theory is beyond

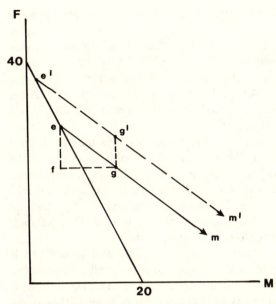

Figure 2.4   Specialization and gains from trade

the scope of this discussion. It is dealt with in detail in most trade theory textbooks. In our illustration, it is enough to note that Betaland is producing at point e and consuming at point g.

By further specializing in the production of F, Betaland could compound its gains from trade. For example, the nation could increase its F production at the expense of M, and move to point e' in Fig. 2.4. Then Betaland could trade down $e'g'm'$ (a consumption possibilities line with the same slope as egm) to point g'. This latter point provides the same amount of M for Betaland consumers but more F than point g. Hence, production specialization from point e to e' will deliver benefits to Betaland's consumers in addition to those provided by the exchange potential that allows this nation to escape its production possibilities curve. Even if the slope of the trading line $e'g'm'$ changes as international deals are made, consumption points like g' are always available as specialization in production occurs.

With this straight-line production possibility curve, continuous specialization would occur until Betaland produced only F and no M. All the M its consumers obtained would come as imports paid for by exports of F.

An exactly comparable argument exists for Alphaland, leading to its specialization in M. In this particular example, with straight-line production possibilities curves, specialization would be complete. Alphaland would produce only M, obtaining its F needs via trade; Betaland would produce only F, using part of it to obtain M by trading. In more complex illustrations, specialization may be partial or complete depending on the overall shape of the nation's production possibilities curves in relation to the international terms of exchange.

Now reconsider the trading world of Alphaland and Betaland reflected in Fig. 2.3. As both nations seek to trade into the unshaded area and as the drive for specialization in production unfolds, Alphaland will become a specialized industrial nation and Betaland will become a specialized agricultural nation. Figure 2.5 reflects this full specialization result and indicates how a final trading equilibrium might appear.

World production is 40 units of F, all supplied by Betaland, and 50 units of M, all supplied by Alphaland. We assert for illustration that a mutually agreeable point of exchange g is found along an international terms-of-exchange line indicated by *am*. Betaland will export 16 units of F to Alphaland, receiving in return 12 imported units of M. Conversely, Alphaland's trading account will show exports of 12 units of M and imports of 16 units of F. This exchange will deliver the trading partners from point *a* to point *g*.

At point g, Alphaland is consuming 38 units of M and 16 units of F. Betaland is consuming 12 units of M and 24 units of F. Naturally, this distribution accounts for the total world production of 50 units of M and 40 units of F.

Note that the move from *a* to *g* is a better trade-off of F for M than either Alphaland or Betaland could make by rearranging its own resources internally. Betaland could get only 8 more units of M internally by releasing resources from 16 units of F; through international trade it can gain 12 M. Similarly, Alphaland could obtain only 12 more units of F internally by shifting resources

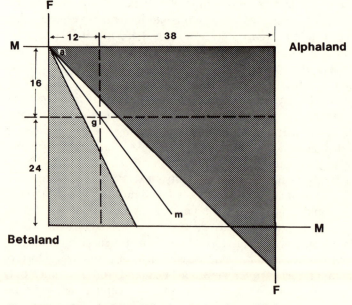

Figure 2.5 Complete specialization and trade equilibrium

and giving up 12 units of M; but on the world market it can get 16 F.

In this example, Betaland has a comparative advantage in agriculture relative to Alphaland. This is because within its own resource structure it can generate 2 units of F for each 1 unit of M it gives up, and Alphaland can get only 1 unit of F for each 1 unit of M it gives up. The reverse argument shows that Alphaland has a comparative advantage in manufactures relative to Betaland. The existence of comparative advantage produces an area of potential trade (an unshaded area) within which *each* nation can make better deals for itself by international exchange than by adjusting its own resources internally.

The principle of comparative advantage is based on differing production conditions among countries. These conditions differ among countries because (1) supplies of productive resources like land, labor, capital goods, and skills available in the work force vary widely from country to country, and costs of using plentiful resources are lower than costs of using scarce resources; (2) different commodities require basic resources in different proportions; (3) most goods can be produced by more than one process, each employing a somewhat different combination of resources; and (4) resources have varying degrees of mobility among countries.

If resources could be transferred easily from one country to another, a major incentive for international trade—differences in relative production costs—would eventually disappear. Yet productive resources such as land and climate are truly fixed, and the migration of people is limited. Consequently, comparative advantage broadly explains most of the world's agricultural trade and much trade in other products. Still, technology, capital, and people do move among nations, changing relative costs and comparative advantage. Hence, patterns of international trade can and do evolve over time. This evolution causes trade problems, interventions by governments, and international trade policy disputes.

GAINS FROM TRADE

If international trade occurs without coercion, people benefit on each side of the transaction. Otherwise, no trade would occur. In addition to narrow commercial motives of individuals, firms, and government agencies, some broader economic effects can be identified as trade develops. The Alphaland-Betaland example illustrates the general motivation for international trade and economywide gains from it. These can be grouped into two categories: those following from the exchange of goods and those stemming from specialization in production.

Exchange

How do individual consumers benefit from international specialization based on comparative advantage? A trade theorist might say that international exchange raises the real income of a trading country. This surely would not convince a steelworker whose job is threatened by foreign steel imports that trade is beneficial. What are the specific benefits of international trade?

International trade is beneficial when it allows buyers access to goods that otherwise would be either unavailable or much more expensive. A large number of tropical products such as coffee, tea, cocoa, bananas, and spices would disappear from supermarket shelves in the United States and Europe if international trade were severely curtailed. Domestic production of such items in heated greenhouses would be extraordinarily costly.

Relatively lower foreign prices also allow consumers to buy more goods with their disposable income. If people can buy imported television sets, textiles, or shoes for significantly lower prices than domestic items of comparable quality, they have in effect raised their incomes. Therefore, lower-priced foreign goods offer consumers a genuine economic opportunity to increase their purchasing power. This is true no matter what the reason for the lower foreign prices. Moreover, these price benefits extend beyond consumer goods. They also are embedded in the imported industrial products and raw materials used to produce final goods domestically at lower prices than otherwise would exist.

Here are some general ideas that virtually all economists would agree with. International trade makes available to consumers a larger and more diverse bundle of goods and services at lower overall prices than does isolation. Compared with isolation, prices of imported goods and their domestic counterparts will be lower. Prices of exported goods may be higher. However, consuming households with specific incomes to allocate will be able to achieve more satisfaction from those incomes in the presence of trade than in its absence.

Specialization

Differences between domestic and international price ratios signal a profitable opportunity to transform domestic goods into foreign goods via exchange. Specialization according to comparative advantage permits a nation to produce more export goods than it wants, then trade them for less costly imported goods from all over the world. This provides a better deal for people as consumers than if everything to be used were produced at home.

Trade theory shows that it is to a country's advantage to specialize, at least partially, in producing goods for which it has relatively lower per-unit costs. National differences in opportunity costs of production determine which goods are exported and which are imported. Thus trade can have a profound impact on a country's economic structure. Trade will stimulate investment in and expansion of industries that produce goods that are comparatively less costly, and it will force the contraction of industries producing comparatively higher-cost items. As industries expand, they will demand inputs and products from other industries. This leads to investment not only in the export sector but elsewhere in the economy. Therefore, the benefits of specialization are not limited only to the expanding export industries.

Resources and investments will move out of less efficient, higher-cost industries and toward expanding sectors. This process may be easy and rapid or painful and slow. As it occurs in a market economy, per-unit costs will tend to rise in expanding industries as less efficient resources are drawn into them, and fall in declining industries as the least efficient resources are forced out. Ultimately, the incentive for further expansion of domestic export production dwindles and disappears. Over time, a country's resources are used most efficiently if they are allocated among industries in order of comparative advantage. This involves specialization.

Distribution of the Gains From Trade

Generally, trade is better for a nation's economy than no trade; yet trade may not be beneficial to all individuals in an economy. And as trade patterns change, the distribution of benefits and the trade-related problems in an economy also change. Most agricultural and industrial goods are produced with numerous raw materials, complex machinery, innovative technology, and skilled management and labor. Each of these inputs must be rewarded for its services—wages for labor, depreciation for machinery, rent for land, royalties for inventions, and returns for ownership and management. The sum of these rewards is the total cost of a product. Unless monopoly or direct government control is involved, the price of a product over time will approach its cost of production.

The reward each class of inputs earns depends on the demand for it and its supply. The demand for any input (land or labor, for example) reflects the total demand for all products using it. Input supplies, however, are often fixed (at least in the short run) and vary widely among countries. Some nations are richly endowed with natural resources such as fertile soil, good climate, or rich mineral deposits. Others have an abundant labor supply. Still others have an elaborate and modern industrial plant. Because resource prices generally reflect relative scarcity, the smaller the supply of a particular input relative to demand, the higher its price and the larger its share in total costs. If producers have some choice over how much of each resource can be used, they will choose a least-cost combination. This means that less expensive resources are employed in place of scarcer, more costly ones.

As international trade develops, trading nations export the services of abundant factors and import the services of relatively scarce factors. As export industries expand because of international trade, the demand for abundant domestic resources increases and so does their value. On the other hand, imports tend to push down the returns for relatively scarce domestic resources. Therefore, there is a tendency for resource prices to be drawn closer together as trade expands. Because of increased production efficiency, the trade-caused loss in income to scarce resources is smaller than the gains to abundant resources. Thus, a country *as a whole* gains from international trade.

Most versions of this elegant and timeless theory of international trade presume that people and productive resources can move from sector to sector and job to job smoothly and easily in response to changes in economic signals and opportunities. In such a well-oiled world, people and capital are always fully employed. Industries that are technically efficient and whose output is in strong world demand set the standards for wages, rents, and dividends that all employers, large and small, must meet.

However, the real world is not so neatly constructed. As economic and technical changes occur both at home and abroad, it is inevitable that old patterns of comparative advantage and relative efficiency will erode. New ones will evolve. Then, previously strong domestic industries may find themselves facing heavy competition from imports. New industries may spring up. Others may begin expanding to meet new international demands. These are clear signals for economic adjustments.

In industries and sectors under strong import competition, firms may be forced to reduce output, lay off workers, and accept lower returns. In the long run, some may even have to close down. The survivors will become more efficient. For the people involved, managers and workers alike, this is a difficult and painful business. For immobile people with highly specialized skills and for land, buildings, and equipment with few alternative uses, there may be virtually no choice. Such capital will continue to be used even at low returns until it wears out, and the people will live with unemployment and despair. So it is not surprising that agricultural and industrial leaders and their political representatives seek protection from imports and onerous adjustments when their traditional markets are threatened. It is this search for protection that lies behind much of the analysis in later chapters of this book.

Jobs and businesses lost to import competition are not often similar to those that open up in other industries, nor are they usually located in the same geographic areas. These factors clog and slow the flow of people and other productive resources away from troubled, inefficient sectors to expanding, efficient ones. There is no general proposition in trade theory that suggests whether or not individual workers, farms, or firms benefit or are hurt by changes in international trade. It all depends on who and where they are. For the economy as a whole, aggregate income and output are higher with more trade than with less trade. But it is a mixed blessing.

SUMMARY

The classical development of trade theory considers the individual nation as the basic economic unit. Mutually beneficial trade can arise among nations because basic production conditions differ from country to country. The differing ability of nations to alter and specialize their mix of outputs by shifting resources internally is the basis of comparative advantage principles. Trade occurs because nations can exploit their comparative advantage to make better deals internationally for goods and services than they can by adjusting resources internally.

Trade allows nations to escape from the constraints of their own production limits. Through international exchange, countries are able to consume a different bundle of goods and services than they actually produce. In general, this opportunity can increase the well-being of each trading nation. Gains from international exchange can be enhanced through specialization in production along lines suggested by comparative advantage principles. Because, in the real world, resources and people are not fully mobile, international trade can cause economic adjustments that are very painful to some people even though society as a whole benefits.

QUESTIONS

2.1   Assume that Nation A has a comparative advantage relative to Nation B in the production of steel versus rice. Explain why and how Nation B has a comparative advantage in the production of rice versus steel.

2.2   Explain and illustrate how a shift away from isolation to international trade can permit a nation to escape from the limitations of its own basic production conditions.

2.3   What are the technical conditions that might keep trading nations from complete specialization in the products for which they display initial comparative advantage? Illustrate.

2.4   Agraria is a country with abundant land, good soil, a productive climate for agriculture, but very few people. As Agraria moves from autarky to the export of farm products, what will happen to land prices and wage rates? Explain your reasoning.

ADDITIONAL READINGS

Agricultural Extension Service, University of Minnesota, St. Paul, Minnesota. 1978. *Speaking of Trade: Its Effect on Agriculture*, Special Report No. 72, Chap. 2. (Basic trade concepts with an agricultural trade flavor.)

Grennes, T. 1984. *International Economics*. Prentice-Hall, Englewood Cliffs, New Jersey, Chaps. 2–4. (A recent, clear, textbook treatment of the basic forces that lie behind comparative advantage and trade.)

Kenen, P. B. 1971. *International Economics*, 3rd ed., Prentice-Hall, Englewood Cliffs, New Jersey, Chaps. 1–2. (A very simple exposition of trade fundamentals, including a statement about why we consider nations as economic units.)

Michaely, M. 1977. *Theory of Commercial Policy*, University of Chicago Press, Chicago, Illinois, Chap. 2. (A more advanced, but nonmathematical, presentation of trade fundamentals.)

Salvatore, D. 1983. *International Economics*, Schaum's Outline Series in Economics, McGraw-Hill Book Co., New York, New York, Chaps. 1–3. (Comparative advantage and gains from trade in outline form with many diagrams.)

Chapter 3

Policy, Protection, and Agriculture

Despite strong theoretical arguments about the broad benefits of freer trade, its application will impose hardship on some industries and people. This sometimes includes farmers, sometimes consumers. Those affected often argue successfully for specific protection against the full force of international competition. These deliberate actions include tariffs, import quotas, domestic content regulations, packing and labeling requirements, sanitary restrictions, variable import levies, export controls, export subsidies, and so on.

This web of specific government decisions is the core of a nation's trade and commercial policy in relation to other nations. A nation's trade policy also can involve other specific actions to encourage and promote foreign trade by improving the legal, financial, and institutional environment within which foreign transactions occur. In addition, the trade policy of a nation reflects its overall attitude about the importance and value of foreign trade in its international behavior.

The general and specific elements of each nation's trade policy interact directly or indirectly with those of other nations in all economic transactions across international borders. Hence, trade policies form the economic buffer between one national economy and another. The main focus of this book will be on the economic aspects of various protective devices that affect trade in agricultural products.

The main reason that a protective web of trade policy evolves within every nation is that the benefits of additional trade usually are spread widely and thinly among numerous individual consumers and vigorous industries. However, the costs and hardships, although smaller in total, almost always are focused on relatively few workers, farms, and industries. These few usually can articulate their problems clearly and press for help. Grasping this fundamental disparity in the incidence of benefits and costs is absolutely essential in understanding the whys and hows of trade policy economics. This is true in both agriculture and industry.

A 2-cent-per-pound increase in the price of sugar caused by an import quota will prompt very few consumers to travel to a nation's capital to protest. Yet an equivalent fall in sugar prices for growers because of increased imports will surely cause sugar producers and their representatives to press strongly and persuasively for protection. Any change in sugar trade simply means more to the average sugar grower than to the average consumer.

In times of growing prosperity and economic expansion, protectionist sentiments shrink and trade expands. In times of recession, general unemployment, or low prices, protectionist sentiments intensify and spread.

REASONS FOR PROTECTION

When farmers, business people, or political leaders call for government-sponsored trade protection on behalf of an industry, they often advance numerous reasons to generate support. These reasons can be classified into a relatively few categories.

Protect a New Industry

Tariffs and quotas often are used to protect new industries. For example, suppose Nation A does not produce cotton but buys it from Nation B. Cost studies show that if A attempted to produce its own cotton, the cost would be higher than B's cotton price. However, the studies may also show that A's cost disadvantage is only a short-term problem. If A somehow could begin cotton production, it might in time be just as efficient or perhaps more efficient than B. But time and money are required to construct efficient irrigation facilities, train producers, and obtain specialized equipment. To enable A to get into cotton production, a tariff might be added to the price of cotton imports from B so that producers in A could begin to compete in the local market. Through the tariff, the consumers of Nation A in effect pay a subsidy to their cotton producers, hoping that someday the new industry will be efficient. Economists call this the "infant industry" argument for protection.

If a fledgling industry has the political power to obtain a protective tariff, it may have the political power to continue it. When this occurs, the infant may never grow up and consumers may find themselves permanently protecting jobs and incomes in a favored industry.

Protect National Security

With trade, specialization in production tends to occur among nations. This tendency might cause a particular domestic industry to shrink below the size considered prudent for strategic reasons. In times of international upheaval or actual war, trade may shrink or stop entirely. If Nation C were dependent on Nation D for the weapons of war, C would be especially vulnerable. Consequently, many nations maintain industries that produce the essentials of war—food and weapons—even though the principles of free trade dictate otherwise.

Maintaining inefficient industries reduces a nation's level of living. However, if a nation might cease to exist by losing a war or being cut off from essentials through hostile action, its citizens might willingly protect industries considered critical to national defense and survival. These often include agriculture, oil, steel, aircraft, and electronics.

Many nations are substantial food importers. Some would be even larger food importers if full international specialization in food production occurred. But most cling to some level of self-sufficiency at least partly for national security reasons. Bitter past experience with food shortages caused by war and trade disruption underpins this policy.

If a particular industry is truly essential to national security, the argument for raising protective trade barriers is reasonable. However, it is always difficult to identify such industries and the size at which they should be maintained.

Protect National Health

The free trade of goods between nations may be restricted for health reasons. The United States, for instance, prohibits the importation of fresh or frozen beef from countries that have a history of foot-and-mouth disease. Likewise, some nations restrict imports of U.S. frozen poultry, fearing infection of their flocks with Newcastle disease. In some countries, metropolitan areas do not permit fluid milk to be sold within their jurisdiction unless the dairy farms, domestic or foreign, have been approved by their own health inspectors.

Clearly, governments are wise to regulate trade in products potentially injurious to public health. However, the public health argument sometimes is used arbitrarily to protect the economic health of some industry, even when there is no health hazard or one no longer exists.

Protect Against "Unfair" Foreign Trade Policy

Most trading nations try to restrict imports of competitive goods when they believe exporters are selling below production costs on international markets and disrupting normal trade. Some export nations occasionally attempt to dispose of surplus agricultural production or capture new markets by offering commodities internationally at prices lower than internal levels. Export subsidies, multiple price schemes, and/or tax advantages may be used for this purpose. Special credit arrangements or price concessions on other export items may also be offered to importers. Selling internationally at prices below domestic production costs is called "dumping."

Consumers of importing nations typically favor the purchase of world market goods offered at low prices. However, producer groups and domestic merchants often succeed in obtaining countervailing duties, quotas, and special restrictions. These are called "antidumping" measures.

Protect Domestic Programs

When a government supports the market price of any commodity above international levels, some form of import control is required to prevent its being swamped by goods from abroad. This is a very difficult problem for many trading nations that provide farm income support through high, guaranteed prices. We will probe this issue in later chapters.

When a national program is established to set market prices above market-clearing or world levels, the amount supplied to that national market, whether from domestic or foreign sources, normally will exceed the amount demanded for consumption. Unless the government operating the program has a bottomless treasury, some means of controlling supplies offered for sale domestically at the support price must be found. Action usually is taken against imports, if there are any, to bring demand and supply into balance at the support price before resorting to unpopular restrictions on domestic producers. But even if some form of internal supply control is used, import controls are needed to keep the program from being inundated from abroad.

Similarly, if the amount supplied by domestic producers at the guaranteed price exceeds domestic use, some form of export enhancement is often pursued.

Protect the Balance of Payments

When a nation's payments to foreigners persistently exceed its earnings from them, the country has an international balance of payments problem. If balance of payments difficulties continue, confidence in the nation's currency and economic strength may be undermined. As a result, downward pressures develop on the value of the nation's currency relative to other currencies.

To stave off currency devaluation, governments often attempt to reduce payments to foreigners by restricting the entry of imported goods. If the nation's export earnings remain the same, the reduction of imports will tend to bring the nation's international payments account toward balance. However, foreign earnings may not stay the same. They may decrease because (1) foreigners, earning less of the restricting nation's currency from imports, may buy less from that nation, turning instead to other suppliers, and (2) foreign governments may retaliate by raising their own trade barriers against products from the restricting nation.

Improve the International Terms of Trade

A large importing nation may be able to force down the world price of a traded product by imposing a tariff on it. This will improve the nation's terms of trade. The theoretical foundation for such a maneuver is based on the ability of the large importer nation to exert monopoly influence on international prices and thereby secure more favorable terms of trade for itself. This motive for imposing a tariff is not primarily for protection, but a domestic industry producing this particular item or its substitute will gain protection indirectly. Economists call this the "optimal" tariff argument.

Provide Revenue

Historically, tariffs were a major source of government revenue for many trading nations. The famous tea import tariffs imposed on the 13 original American colonies had no protective value. They were simply a tax on colonial tea consumers. The revenues went to the British government.

Tariffs and export taxes can be attractive government revenue sources because of the relative ease with which they can be collected. This is especially so for numerous developing countries, since income or profit taxes are difficult to collect. Export taxes on tropical agricultural products and raw materials are still widely employed by many less-developed exporters. However, most developed countries now levy tariffs mainly to protect domestic industries rather than to raise revenue. For example, United States tariff revenues in 1982 were only 1.4 percent of all government receipts.

Protect against Painful Economic Adjustment

As economic changes occur around the world, it is inevitable that familiar patterns of comparative and absolute advantage will erode, and new ones will evolve. Previously strong and vigorous domestic industries may find themselves facing heavy competition from imports of foreign goods. This is a clear signal for some economic adjustment.

If the increased import flow and the resulting downward pressure on domestic prices and sales are not caused by dumping by foreign sellers, some domestic producers may be forced either to leave the affected industry, accept lower returns, or become more efficient. For the people involved, this is often a difficult and painful choice. For some resources like highly specialized buildings and equipment there may be no choice.

Thus it is not at all surprising that industrial leaders and their representatives first seek government protection when imports threaten traditional domestic markets. Although other reasons, such as those mentioned earlier, may be presented and argued, the desire to avoid harsh economic adjustment almost always lies behind the drive for new or stricter import controls. This is especially true in agriculture and basic industries of trading nations. Resources in these industries are traditionally less mobile than elsewhere. Moreover, powerful economic and technical changes quite apart from foreign competition already may be at work within these industries.

Export nations sometimes intervene in international trade to protect their domestic consumers from high prices and vigorous foreign demand for important locally produced items. Export taxes or quotas are the usual devices for such protection. These measures bottle up available supplies in the internal economy and discourage foreign sales. Although domestic consumers are thus shielded from competition by eager foreign buyers, domestic producers face lower prices too and may reduce future output.

AGRICULTURE'S NICHE IN TRADE POLICY

Almost all nations that can afford it, and some that cannot, channel special attention and public expenditure to their food and agriculture sectors, sometimes to farmers and sometimes to consumers. This often comes in the form of deliberate action to tip the scales of the domestic or international market in favor of local producers or consumers. Sometimes the purse strings of public expenditure may be loosened in favor of farmers. On the other hand, special taxes may be invoked to generate government revenue from sales of farm and food products. What is it about agriculture that makes it a prime candidate for government intervention, domestically and across international borders?

The reasons are political, social, cultural, and economic. Of course they are all entwined closely in the web of public affairs, but a rough separation might be made between political-social reasons and economic reasons. First among the political-social reasons is that food and fiber are absolute necessities in any society. A modern government that cannot guarantee its citizens reasonably adequate food and clothing at affordable costs is not long in power. This strategic role of food and fiber pushes governments toward fostering a healthy farm industry in both peace and war. For example, bitter memories of food shortages during and after World Wars I and II give several European nations and Japan an incentive to subsidize their farm sectors and thereby keep them much larger than they otherwise would be.

In most developed nations, both farm and rural populations have dwindled to less than 15 percent of the total as people are drawn into other more rapidly growing fields of employment. Yet the political influence of rural producers and their representatives usually has remained strong enough to prevent a rapid erosion of protective programs begun when the number of producers was larger. This generalization seems true under widely different political systems. Partly it is because of slowness in adjusting political representation to dwindling numbers of rural residents, and partly it is because political power in many societies is land-based to some extent. In the United States, for instance, each state has two senators no matter what its population or geographic size.

Some public programs on behalf of agriculture have roots in a special, often mystical, relationship between people and land that pervades virtually every political or social system. The land-people question remains significant in modern agriculture even though it carries little weight in other industries. In one nation it may appear in policies designed to foster a system of small, fully owned family farms. In another, it may be seen in programs to ensure ultimate public ownership, and perhaps direct control, of agricultural and pastoral resources.

A majority of today's city dwellers around the world are at most two or three generations away from life on the land. In large numbers, they share a nostalgic view that much of rural life is somehow more fulfilling and worthy than urban existence. This in turn has led to their taking a rather charitable general view of public protection for agriculture. However, in the modern era of rising food prices, growing consumer activism, and disenchantment with public programs of all kinds, it would be an error to overestimate this phenomenon. It is also a mistake to ignore it entirely.

There are a number of economic reasons why agricultural industries are continual candidates for public protection. Three major reasons are stability problems, income problems, and foreign trade problems. It is widely, though not unanimously, agreed that markets for most agricultural products are more unstable than necessary for efficient use of resources and efficient management of buyers' expenditures. Sizable price, output, and income fluctuations occur in agriculture because of notorious inelasticities of demand and supply, uncertainties of foreign markets, and the vagaries of weather, insects, and disease peculiar to farming. Most legislation to protect farmers and most programs dealing with the marketing of agricultural products usually have the term "stabilization" attached to them somewhere. While it is virtually impossible to disentangle stabilization motives from other motives in any policy, the objective is almost always a strong one.

In most nations, long-term growth in farm income has not kept pace with income growth in nonrural sectors, even after instability is accounted for. Protection programs to help redress this tendency are typical in most developed nations. These measures are many and varied. They operate by influencing the markets in which producers sell their outputs and purchase their supplies, or they add financial payments directly to the farm income flow.

Few nations are completely self-sufficient in the production of food and fiber. Some are net importers, some are net exporters. Rightly or wrongly, policymakers in net importing nations often visualize the use of foreign exchange for buying food and agricultural raw materials as unnecessary, wasteful, or dangerous to national security. So protection programs may be undertaken to promote the growth of import-substituting agricultural enterprises. Similarly, agricultural exporting nations may deliberately promote the production and export of agricultural goods to stimulate their domestic farm economies.

The full array of reasons for, and the goals sought by, agricultural protection programs are seldom clear-cut or carefully defined. In most nations these programs are begun and sustained by political action. Therefore they are subject to all the mixed motives, compromises, and cross-currents of interest that political action entails. Yet there can be no doubt that agriculture occupies a special niche in the public policy arena all around the world. Special treatment of and intervention in agricultural food and fiber markets extend naturally from the domestic scene to the nexus of international transactions among countries.

ANALYSIS OF PROTECTION AND INTERVENTION

Most of the rest of this book involves discussion and economic analysis of various protective devices that governments adopt in agricultural and other markets. In Chap. 4 we will develop a partial equilibrium framework to conduct these analyses. Manipulation and rearrangement of that basic system will allow us to examine the economic impacts of specific trade policy schemes. We will emphasize effects on prices, production, consumption, trade, and income. We will attempt to identify gainers and losers in both the domestic and international setting.

Mostly, our point of reference will be the individual national economy conducting specific, protective, or other trade policies. Our focus generally will not be global even though we examine important international implications.

SUMMARY

The web of specific government decisions about the conduct of international trade is the core of an individual nation's trade policy. A central aspect of trade policy in virtually all nations is the protection of some industries or sectors from the full force of international competition. Numerous reasons for trade protection are advanced by advocates—some sensible from the whole society's viewpoint, others not. Protection from painful economic adjustment signaled by trade flows is the most common root cause of direct governmental intervention in trade. Most protective measures arise because the benefits of additional trade are spread widely and thinly among many individuals in a nation, but the costs are pinpointed on relatively few firms and workers.

Agricultural trade occupies a special niche in the trade policy arena. The essential nature of food and fiber to human welfare, the particular biological character of agricultural production, and the long-term behavior of prices and incomes in agriculture lead to direct and continuous government intervention all over the globe in agricultural markets including foreign trade.

QUESTIONS

3.1 List the obvious conflicts and inconsistencies in the trade policy of a nation with which you are familiar—say, the United States, Japan, Brazil, etc.

3.2 Explain how you would design an effective and fair trade policy to benefit both an "infant industry" and society as a whole.

3.3 How would you go about deciding what the minimum level of national food self-sufficiency should be in a nation that imports large amounts of agricultural products?

3.4 Imagine that you are the minister of agriculture for a large, diverse country. Develop a list of sensible reasons why the farmers in your nation might qualify for special policy attention and protection by the government. What other broader considerations would likely be of concern to the national president or prime minister?

ADDITIONAL READINGS

Agricultural Extension Service, University of Minnesota, St. Paul, Minnesota. 1978. *Speaking of Trade: Its Effect on Agriculture*, Special Report No. 72, Chaps. 1–3. (Policy, protection, and trade in agriculture, with emphasis on the United States.)

Houck, J. P., and Kendrick, J. G. 1968. *The Protectionist Mood and Midwest Agricultural Trade*, North Central Extension Publication 24 and University of Minnesota Extension Bulletin No. 355 (October 1968). (Free trade versus protectionism is the central topic here, with emphasis on the whys of protectionist policies.)

McCalla, A. F. 1969. Protectionism in international agricultural trade, 1850-1968, *Agricultural History*, 43(3):329–344. (A long-run view of how and why agricultural trade is a prime candidate for government intervention.)

Sorenson, V. L. 1975. *International Trade Policy: Agriculture and Development*, International and Business Studies, Michigan State University, East Lansing, Michigan, Chap. 4. (Roots of trade policy and policy conflicts in agriculture.)

Tontz, R. L. 1977. *Foreign Agricultural Trade Policy of the United States, 1776-1976*, Economic Research Service, U.S. Department of Agriculture, Washington, D.C. (January 10, 1977). (A long historical view of the agricultural trade policy of the United States, including domestic policies and international agreements.)

Warley, T. K. 1976. Agriculture in international economic relations, *American J. of Agricultural Economics* 58(5):820–830 (December 1976). (A professional but nontechnical statement about how agricultural policy issues affect and are affected by international trade.)

Chapter 4

The Partial Equilibrium Setting for Trade Policy Analysis

For the rest of this book, the major analytical tools will be partial equilibrium constructions. We will be in the world of demand and supply functions. Our main emphasis will be on price, production, income, and trade effects of policy decisions as applied to individual agricultural commodities or commodity groups. In partial equilibrium analysis, we limit our view to a specific sector of the domestic and international economy, as we hold other things constant, at least conceptually.

A disadvantage of this approach is that it suppresses interactions between commodities that are actually linked together by substitution and competition. Such interactions certainly can be considered, but this involves extra analytical steps. For the analysis of trade policy principles, the partial equilibrium regime has numerous advantages. It is simpler to understand and manipulate, especially for people with modest experience in using economic theory and mathematics. For specific trade policy schemes and interventions, partial equilibrium analysis provides sharp results that highlight important differences among policy measures.

Most real-world policy interventions are targeted at specific commodity problems. Tariffs, quotas, and export subsidies, for example, are almost always designed either to assist or exploit a particular producing sector. Analysis of that direct impact is important. Partial equilibrium analysis is the most useful approach for assessing direct and immediate economic impacts, even though we should not ignore the broader, more diffuse results of policy decisions.

Since our goal will be logical inquiry and not statistical measurement, our analytical approach will be static. In this context, the term "static" does not mean "changeless." It means "timeless." That is, the passage of calendar time will not be specifically accounted for except when we distinguish between short-run and long-run effects. Our static demand and supply functions will be short-run relationships. They illustrate how quantities demanded and supplied change in response to price signals after sufficient time has elapsed to allow both production and consumption to adjust without fundamental changes occurring in the sector's resource base.

Static partial equilibrium analysis does not attempt to exhaust reality. It is an abstract and stylized form of reasoning within which extraneous influences, important as they may be in the real world, are held at bay momentarily. The purpose is to see as clearly as possible how individual trade policy decisions influence the market environment. The basic system we discuss in this chapter is the foundation for virtually everything that follows.

ISOLATION EQUILIBRIUM: AUTARKY

We consider the nation as an economic unit. To avoid unneeded complexity in our analysis, let us assume we can assert that the demand function D in Fig. 4.1 is the horizontal sum of all short-run, independent, individual demand functions in Nation A for some well-defined agricultural product q at a particular marketing level, such as wholesale. It is the schedule of the total quantities demanded of q at various prices within Nation A holding other prices, incomes, and tastes and preferences steady.

Similarly, let us assert that S is the horizontal sum of numerous individual, independent, short-run supply functions for q in Nation A at the same marketing level as for D. The function S is a schedule of the quantities of q supplied at various prices after some short-run production adjustments are made. To form S, we also hold other prices, input supply schedules, and technology constant. Whether this supply function's slope is steep (inelastic) or shallow (elastic) depends on the nature of the production process as well as the number and character of production inputs we allow to be variable. We can leave these details somewhat vague in the context of our abstract reasoning because we want to illuminate general principles. However, they would need to be specified in any particular, real case.

We will also assume that numerous buyers are captured in D and numerous sellers in S. This will allow us the luxury of conducting our analyses within the domain of atomistic or perfect competition. Once we grasp the essentials of competitive results in trade policy analysis, we are equipped to alter the assumptions to accommodate various market power and imperfectly competitive arrangements. Almost everywhere, agricultural producers and consumers are numerous enough so that atomistic economic behavior within national food and fiber markets is not a seriously misleading assumption, especially for raw

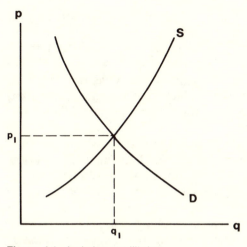

Figure 4.1 Isolation equilibrium

or semiprocessed farm products. Of course, this atomistically competitive assumption does not extend to individual nations, as economic units, in their transactions with other nations. More about this later.

It is tempting to assert that the intersection of D and S in Fig. 4.1 has economic meaning. However, we first need to establish two further conditions before doing that—(1) none of the buyers captured in D can obtain the product q from anyone other than the sellers captured in S, and (2) none of the sellers captured in S can dispose of q except to buyers in D. If these two conditions hold, the intersection of D and S is the familiar equilibrium price and quantity solution of economic textbooks. In Fig. 4.1, this solution is p_I and q_I. If no dealings with foreign buyers or sellers occur, p_I and q_I are an isolation equilibrium solution for Nation A. Such isolation may be deliberate, enforced by stringent trade policy measures at the borders. It may be the consequence of distance and prohibitive transportation costs for q. Or it may be that q is so highly perishable that international exchange is not feasible.

When a country deliberately seeks isolation from international exchange across many important sectors, the result is called "autarky." Under full autarky, isolation equilibrium prices prevail throughout the economy.

INTERNATIONAL TRADE

Autarky Relaxed

Suppose international trade in q is possible (or feasible) for buyers and sellers in Nation A. Let us imagine that a previous policy of autarky in q is relaxed—no trade barriers remain. Also suppose that the international price of q, adjusted to the geographic location of Nation A, is available to all buyers and sellers and is higher than p_I. In this case, sellers in Nation A will wish to earn the higher international price and will divert supplies to the world market. This will short the domestic market, driving prices inside A up toward the international price. Nation A will become an exporter of q.

If the international price is lower than p_I, buyers in A will turn to foreign sellers. This will cause a glut of domestic production on the internal q market, pushing domestic prices in Nation A down toward the international price. Nation A will become an importer of q.

We depict this tendency to import or export in Fig. 4.2, which elaborates and clarifies the trade aspects of Fig. 4.1 but adds nothing fundamentally new. Fig. 4.2a is the same as Fig. 4.1. Fig. 4.2b illustrates possible conditions in the international market. In Fig. 4.2b we measure exports (q_x) to the right of 0 and imports (q_m) to the left.

When international prices are above p_I, Nation A will tend to export q. More will be supplied by domestic producers than will be demanded by domestic buyers as internal prices rise. The function ES in Fig. 4.2b is the "excess supply" function for q at various international prices above p_I when trade is permitted by Nation A. It is the horizontal difference between S and D, measuring the amount of q supplied for export (Q_x). The higher the international price, the more is supplied by the producers in A and the less is demanded by domestic users. Hence, the ES curve slopes positively.

When international prices are below p_I, Nation A will tend to import q. Less will be supplied by domestic producers than will be demanded by domestic buyers as internal prices fall. The function ED in Fig. 4.2b is the "excess demand" function for q at various international prices below p_I when trade is permitted by Nation A. It is the horizontal difference between D and S, measuring the amount of q demanded for import (q_m). The lower the international price, the less is supplied by the producers in A and the more is demanded

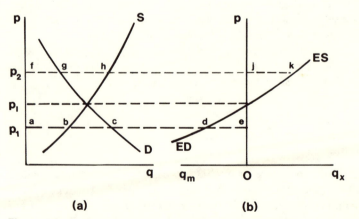

Figure 4.2 Deriving excess demand and supply functions

by domestic users. Hence, the *ED* curve slopes negatively if we consider imports as positive quantities.

If the international price should happen to equal p_I, Nation A will neither import nor export product *q*. If the international price is p_1, the amount *ac* in Fig. 4.2*b* will be demanded by domestic buyers but only *ab* will be produced locally. The amount *bc* will need to be imported. Import amount *bc* is exactly equal to *de* shown in Fig. 4.2*b*. At international price p_2, *fh* will be produced by suppliers in A, but only *fg* will be purchased by domestic users, leaving *gh* to be exported. This export amount *gh* is exactly equal to *jk* shown in Fig. 4.2*b*. The entire function *ED-ES* in Fig. 4.2*b* shows the tendency of Nation A to import less and less along *ED* as world prices rise from very low levels toward isolation equilibrium and then for A to emerge as an exporter as prices rise beyond p_I. Nation A will export more and more along *ES* as international prices climb.

Elasticity of Excess Demand and Supply Functions

The *ED-ES* function is generally less steep and more price responsive than either the domestic demand curve (*D*) or the domestic supply curve (*S*). An increase in the international price for *q*, if it is transmitted to the domestic market, causes a change in either the amount demanded for import (along the *ED* segment) or the amount supplied for export (along the *ES* segment). In the first instance, the amount demanded for import will fall; in the second, the amount supplied for export will rise. In each case, the change in trade volume is because the amount supplied domestically rises and the amount demanded domestically falls. These production and consumption changes combine to generate proportionately larger trade changes.

For those who like to think in elasticity terms, the price elasticity of the *ED-ES* function is larger (in absolute value) than the absolute price elasticity of either the domestic *S* or *D* functions. In fact, the following relationships are easy to develop. Let

$$q_T = q_S - q_D \tag{4.1}$$

where q_S is the domestic quantity supplied, q_D is the domestic quantity demanded, and q_T is the quantity to be traded. If q_T is positive, exports are indicated; if q_T is negative, imports are indicated. The systematic relationship between q_T and price *p* is the *ED-ES* curve. If the symbol Δ is taken to mean "change in," we can write

$$\frac{\Delta q_T}{\Delta p} = \frac{\Delta q_S}{\Delta p} - \frac{\Delta q_D}{\Delta p} \tag{4.2}$$

This relationship says that the change in q_T per unit change in price is equal to the difference in the corresponding changes of q_S and q_D per unit price change. Price elasticities can be expressed, in general, as

$$e = \frac{\Delta q}{\Delta p} \cdot \frac{p}{q} \tag{4.3}$$

In this context, Eq. 4.3 indicates that the price elasticity (e) is the percentage change in q associated with a 1 percent increase in p. Then

$$e_E = \frac{\Delta q_T}{\Delta p} \cdot \frac{p}{q_T} \tag{4.4}$$

$$e_S = \frac{\Delta q_S}{\Delta p} \cdot \frac{p}{q_S} \tag{4.5}$$

and

$$e_D = \frac{\Delta q_D}{\Delta p} \cdot \frac{p}{q_D} \tag{4.6}$$

where e_E, e_S, and e_D are the price elasticities of the *ED-ES*, *S*, and *D* curves respectively.

After some rudimentary algebra, Eqs. 4.4, 4.5, and 4.6 combined with 4.2 provide the following relationship:

$$e_E = e_S \frac{q_S}{q_T} - e_D \frac{q_D}{q_T} \tag{4.7}$$

Since the domestic demand elasticity e_D is generally negative and e_S is usually positive, and since q_T can be plus or minus, Eq. 4.7 can be restated as

$$|e_E| = |e_S| \cdot \left| \frac{q_S}{q_T} \right| + |e_D| \cdot \left| \frac{q_D}{q_T} \right| \tag{4.8}$$

Thus the absolute price elasticity value of *ED-ES* is a weighted sum of the domestic demand and supply elasticities taken without regard to sign.
The weights are the ratios of the domestic supply or demand to the volume traded. The actual elasticity of the *ED* segment will be negative, while that of the *ES* segment will be positive.

If we consider the *ED* segment where imports are involved q_D/q_T will be absolutely equal to or greater than 1.0, ensuring that e_E will be absolutely larger than e_D. Along the *ES* segment involving exports, q_S/q_T will be equal to or greater than 1.0, ensuring that e_E will be absolutely larger than e_S.

Shift in Trade Status

The *ED-ES* function illustrates how Nation A can change from an importer to an exporter of *q* as prices change and nothing happens to alter the location or shape of the domestic demand and supply relationships. It is also illuminating to consider how a shift in a nation's trade status can occur even if international prices do not change.

Consider Fig. 4.3. The initial situation is reflected by *D*, *S*, and *ED-ES*. At the international price of p_1, Nation A exports an amount equal to *bc* in Fig. 4.3*b*. Suppose the price remains constant, but the domestic supply function shifts strongly to the left from *S* to *S'*; less will be produced in Nation A at each price. This could be the result of a drought or serious weather disturbance, like a storm or a flood, that destroys farms, orchards, or other producing facilities.

As the supply function shifts to the left, the *ED-ES* function also will shift in the same direction to *ED'-ES'*. The isolation equilibrium price will increase from point *d* to point *e* in Fig. 4.3*b*. If price remains at p_1 (or lower than *e*), Nation A will shift from being an exporter of *q* to being an importer of *q*. At p_1, the amount *ab* will be imported.

Numerous other examples could be constructed easily, but the point is clear. Under plausible combinations of price change and/or shifts in domestic production and demand conditions, changes in trade status from exporter to importer or vice versa can readily occur.

A Two-Nation Trading Regime

Imagine that Nation A and Nation B comprise the relevant trading world for *q*. Figure 4.4 reflects this situation. This diagram is an elaboration of previous figures, with Nation B's domestic demand and supply curves illustrated in Fig. 4.4*c*. The international market (Fig. 4.4*b*) now includes the *ED-ES* functions

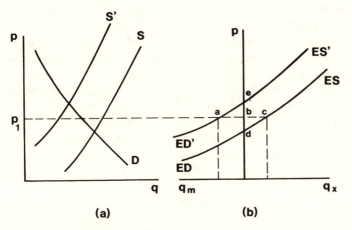

Figure 4.3 Trade status shift

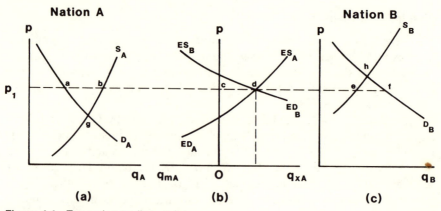

Figure 4.4 Two-nation trading regime

for Nations A and B, appropriately labeled. In addition, the horizontal axis of Fig. 4.4*b* also carries quantity labels from Nation A's point of view. Since only two nations are involved, A's exports (q_{xA}) must equal B's imports. If A were an importer, its imports (q_{mA}) would equal B's exports.

At this point we will not introduce the possibility of a changeable exchange rate between the currencies of A and B. Assume that the currency values are fixed in relation to each other and that the particular exchange rate is 1 for 1. Thus we can use p as the world price as well as the price measure in each country.

Isolation equilibrium is at point g in A and point h in B. Imagine an initial autarky regime. Since the price at h is higher than the price at g, sellers in A will seek buyers in B, and buyers in B will seek supplies from A, once trade is permitted. Trade will begin to flow from A to B. This process will cause an immediate shortage in Nation A and a market glut in Nation B. The price in Nation A will tend to rise and the price in Nation B will tend to fall.

As prices rise in A, less will be demanded domestically and more will be supplied—the excess supply volume of Nation A will increase along ES_A. As prices fall in B, more will be demanded domestically and less will be supplied—the excess demand volume of Nation B will increase along ED_B. This process will continue as long as prices are higher in Nation B than in Nation A. Trade will expand until prices are equalized in both nations, ignoring transportation and other transfer costs. Where prices are equal in both nations, there will be no advantage to traders in either country to expand international sales or purchases. This tendency for prices to equalize across freely trading areas is sometimes called "the law of one price."

In Fig. 4.4, the value of p_1 is the price at which the quantity of exports from A—namely, ab—is exactly equal to the quantity of imports into *B*—namely, *ef*. The quantity of trade, its direction, and the equilibrium international price are registered in Fig. 4.4*b* as the intersection of ED_A-ES_A and ES_B-

ED_B. Note that the equilibrium price p_1 lies between the two isolation prices and that the volume of trade cd is equal to ab and ef.

Any shift in the domestic supply or demand functions in A or B will shift the position of the excess demand-supply function of that nation and change the equilibrium international price and quantity traded. It is instructive to redraw Fig. 4.4, then experiment with some hypothetical shifts, tracing their implications for trade and domestic market adjustments.

Transfer Costs

Next consider what happens if we include transportation costs or other transaction charges that may apply as goods are transferred from A to B. Figure 4.5 illustrates this. Let the total of these costs be equal to the value mn. The domestic prices in the two nations in equilibrium will then differ by this amount.

The price in Nation A (p_A) is mn units lower than the price in Nation B (p_B). Thus, $p_A + mn = p_B$. The equilibrium position in Fig. 4.5 is located by finding the trade volume at which the difference in the two prices is exactly equal to mn. This is Oq_1. If the transfer costs should increase, the price difference will widen and trade volume will fall. If the transfer costs should increase up to or beyond the value gh, trade will shrink to zero because transfer costs then will equal or exceed the difference between the two isolation prices. No incentive would exist for trade in this product. So even if isolation prices differ for a particular product, trade need not occur. It will not occur if transfer costs are so high that traders cannot take profitable advantage of potential price differences.

Note that the introduction of transfer costs boosts the price in B and lowers it in A compared with the no-cost equilibrium at d. The differential impact on prices in each of the two nations depends on the slope (or price elasticity) of the respective ED_B or ES_A functions. If ED_B is steeper (or more price inelastic) than ES_A, p_B will increase more than p_A will fall. Conversely, if ES_A is steeper than ED_B, p_A will fall further than p_B will rise. Thus the incidence of

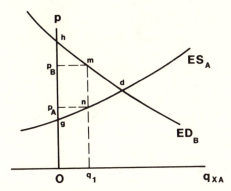

Figure 4.5 Including transfer costs in international pricing

price changes in response to transfer cost changes between trading nations is dictated by the relative steepness of excess supply and demand functions, which in turn depend on domestic demand and supply elasticities. The lower the elasticities, the larger the internal price changes.

NATION A IN A MULTINATION TRADING REGIME

We need to expand our view of the trading world around Nation A. We must be able to visualize a trading regime larger than just one other country. Moreover, the analytical difference for our purpose involves only a relatively modest adjustment of the Nation A versus Nation B situation of the previous section.

We can consider Nation B as a composite of all other trading nations in the world. To follow that line of reasoning, let the curve D_B in Fig. 4.4 be the sum of all *excess* demand curves of importing nations (countries that import q when prices are in the relevant range). The amount demanded along D_B is the total amount of q demanded for import by world buyers at various prices. Similarly, let the function S_B in Fig. 4.4 be the sum of *excess* supply curves of *other* exporting nations, excluding Nation A. The amount supplied along S_B is then the amount supplied to world markets by *other* exporters at various prices.

In this setting, the function ED_B in Fig. 4.4 becomes the excess demand curve for the "rest of the world" faced by Nation A for product q. The quantity $ab = cd = ef$ is the amount supplied by Nation A to the rest of the world. This quantity is at the intersection of ES_A and ED_B, where the latter function reflects the world excess demand for q faced by Nation A.

It should be clear that this discussion, like previous illustrations, can be reversed so that Nation B can be considered as a single importer and Nation A can be viewed as the rest of the world in composite. If Nation B is the focal point, ED_B can be interpreted as the schedule of imports demanded by B from the rest of the world at various prices. Similarly, if B is the focal point, ES_A can be interpreted as the schedule of exports supplied to B by the rest of the world at various prices after considering the potential consumption of other, competing importers.

In the analyses to follow, we will generally consider that an importing nation faces an excess supply from the rest of the world considered as an aggregate. We will usually label it $ES(R)$. Likewise, we usually visualize an exporting nation as facing an aggregate excess demand curve from the rest of the world. We will usually label it $ED(R)$.

LARGE- VERSUS SMALL-NATION EFFECTS

When we consider a single country in relation to the rest of the trading world, it is sensible to distinguish between two important cases. These are whether we consider the export or import nation under consideration to be "large" or "small" in relation to the total traded volume of the product in question. The matter hinges on the size of the individual nation's purchases or sales in relation to total volume marketed in the trading world.

A nation is large if potential changes in either its exports or imports are sizable enough to cause the relevant world price to change. A nation is small if its potential trade volume in relation to the world market is so small that its possible effects on international prices can be safely ignored. This distinction is comparable to a firm's situation in economic theory. A "small firm" is an atomistic competitor, a "large firm" is an imperfect competitor. The former can have no effect on prices it faces by altering its purchases or sales; the latter does.

A large export nation will face a negatively sloping *ED* function from the rest of the world. Changes in its exports will affect the international price. A small export nation will face a flat, horizontal *ED* function positioned at the world price. Changes in its export volume will not affect the international price.

A large import nation will face a positively sloping *ES* function for the rest of the world. By altering its imports, this nation can influence the world price. A small import nation will face a flat *ES* function positioned at the world price. It cannot influence world price by adjusting its imports.

The large-nation case is more general because we can always imagine that the relevant excess demand or supply curve facing the trading nation could become more and more price elastic (flatter) until the small-nation situation is achieved. Another way to visualize this distinction is shown in Fig. 4.6. Imagine that our hypothetical Nation A faces an excess demand/excess supply function for the rest of the world that spans a vast range of potential imports and exports of q; this function is *ED(R)-ES(R)* in Fig. 4.6.

Nation A is a small potential importer or exporter in the ranges ecompassed by ED_{A1} and ED_{A2} and by ES_{A1} and ES_{A2} respectively. Changes in import or export volumes by A in these neighborhoods have no discernible ef-

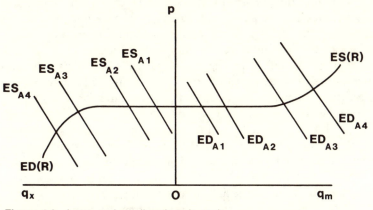

Figure 4.6 Large and small nations in trade

fects on world price. On the other hand, when Nation A is large enough on the international scene so that either ED_{A3} or ES_{A3} is relevant, it is a large trader. This is because a movement from ED_{A3} to ED_{A4} or from ES_{A3} to ES_{A4} will affect world prices. The $ED(R)-ES(R)$ function is sloped in those neighborhoods. An increase in import demand by Nation A from ED_{A3} to ED_{A4} will pull up world prices as A's buyers bid international supplies away from other importers. An increase in export supply by Nation A from ES_{A3} to ES_{A4} will push down world prices as additional exports from A's sellers push their way onto world markets.

TRADE AND SUBSTITUTES

Our partial equilibrium system of analysis is easiest to use when we regard imports as products that are virtually identical to domestically produced items. If imports and local products are identical, they are perfect substitutes for each other. But it is also helpful to recognize that virtually all the conclusions to be drawn from partial equilibrium analysis with perfect substitutes are also applicable for imperfect substitutes or differentiated products.

Imported corn and domestic corn, for instance, may be broadly similar except that imported corn may contain more protein. This difference makes the two products somewhat dissimilar but highly competitive with each other as a feedstuff for livestock. This feature of substitutability allows us to extend our partial equilibrium line of reasoning one or more stages further.

Let Fig. 4.7 illustrate the domestic demand and supply functions for product z in Nation A. Assume that z is a uniquely domestic product, neither imported nor exported. Imagine that the isolation equilibrium price for z at some initial point in time is given by the intersection of D_z and S_z at point a. Assume that some other product q is a substitute for z—not a perfect substitute but a closely related item in consumption like imported versus domestic cars or corn.

In partial equilibrium theory, functions like D_z and S_z are drawn with prices of other related products (like q) held constant. Now imagine that imports of q fall from the initial situation and, as a result, the price of q inside Nation A increases. Since q and z are substitutes, theory tells us that the whole demand curve for z will shift to the right—to D_{z1} in Fig. 4.7. This is because at least some buyers of q are prepared to switch to z if the relative price of q with respect to z increases. This increase in the demand for z will tend to bid up its price and volume sold, say to point b.

Similarly, a glut of imported q will drive down its price and shift the demand curve of z to the left—to D_{z2}. As the relative price of q falls, at least some z buyers are prepared to switch to q. This fall in the demand for z will press down its price and market volume, say to point c. Thus, changes in the prices of import goods, through the links of commodity substitution, will drag along prices of their domestic substitutes in the same direction.

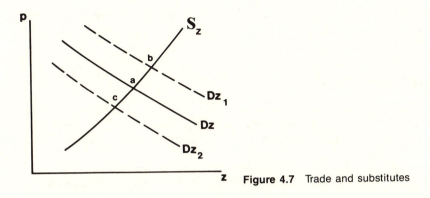

Figure 4.7 Trade and substitutes

A completely symmetrical argument can be framed for the situation in which q is an export good linked by substitution in use to the uniquely domestic good z. This line of argument is left for the reader to develop.

SUMMARY

This chapter lays out the basic partial equilibrium framework to be used for the economic analysis of various import and export trade policy schemes. The analytical framework introduced in this chapter is capable of dealing with both import and export situations. Adjustments in both domestic and international markets are highlighted. The major emphasis in this approach is on the effects and adjustments within the individual nation initiating a particular trade intervention. However, world market implications are not ignored.

Partial equilibrium supply and demand functions are the primary tools of analysis. Hence, the focus of attention is on individual products and commodity groups that can be traded internationally or that are relatively close substitutes for them.

QUESTIONS

4.1 The nation of Industria has long been a butter-importing country. However, dwindling demand for butter inside the nation has recently caused Industria to become a small exporter of butter to the world market. Illustrate this development with partial equilibrium diagrams.

4.2 Illustrate with diagrams how a bumper wheat crop in the large exporting nation of Grainland will drive down the world price of wheat.

4.3 Describe the effects on trade and prices in the world citrus fruit market if ocean freight rates increase dramatically. Consider implications for both exporters and importers of citrus fruit.

4.4 The tropical nation of Solaria has limited agricultural land. For instance, it can produce bananas for export or plantains for domestic food use; there is no foreign trade in plantains. Bananas and plantains are not very close substitutes in consumption, but they are in production. In recent years, international banana prices have been increasing. Illustrate and discuss how this development affects the domestic market for plantains.

ADDITIONAL READINGS

Agricultural Extension Service, University of Minnesota, St. Paul, Minnesota. 1978. *Speaking of Trade: Its Effect on Agriculture*, Special Report No. 72, Chap. 3. (This chapter includes an exposition of the partial equilibrium economics of international trade.)

Bressler, R. G., and King, R. A. 1970. *Markets, Prices, and Interregional Trade*, John Wiley & Sons, New York, New York, Chaps. 4 and 5. (Though not an international trade text, this book is one of the best sources for the partial equilibrium economics of pricing and exchange in separated markets.)

Grennes, T. 1984. *International Economics*. Prentice-Hall, Englewood Cliffs, New Jersey, Chap. 3. (This chapter outlines the partial equilibrium economics of excess demand and supply and links it to general equilibrium reasoning.)

Sorenson, V. L. 1975. *International Trade Policy: Agriculture and Development*, International and Business Studies, Michigan State University, East Lansing, Michigan, Chap. 3. (A short exposition of both partial and general equilibrium exchange in international markets.)

Part Two

Protection
by Importers

Free trade, they concede, is very well as a principle, but it is never quite time for its adoption.

Ralph Waldo Emerson

Chapter 5

Tariffs and Quotas

Tariffs and import quotas are the meat and potatoes of protective trade policy. They are the traditional mechanisms by which governments of importing nations intervene to shield their domestic producers from foreign competition. In addition, tariffs may generate sizable amounts of government revenue. Quotas, too, can be administered and allocated to create government revenue. Our main focus here will be on the protective rather than public finance aspects of tariffs and quotas, although we will not ignore the revenue side. Because they either raise the internal price of imported goods or stint the domestic market of foreign supplies, tariffs and quotas protect domestic producers of the affected items from the full force of international competition.

An import tariff is a tax on the affected foreign item, levied as it passes into the domestic economy. An import quota is a physical limit on the amount of the affected foreign item that can be imported within a specified time period. In practice, tariffs and quotas can be and are calculated, applied, and administered in endlessly complex ways. They can be used separately or together. Even though governments show amazing ingenuity in fashioning intricate tariff and quota schemes to protect domestic producers, the basic economics is relatively straightforward.

In this chapter we will look closely at the direct effects of relatively simple tariffs and quotas. Most of the common elaborations and complications do not materially alter the economic consequences of these two basic policy mechanisms. Although substantial public funds may be generated by tariffs or quotas, we will assume generally that this is not their central purpose. Their main goal here will be to elevate internal prices of the affected goods relative to international prices.

First, we will consider the economics of fixed and ad valorem tariffs applied by both small and large trading nations. Next, we will look at the economics of import quotas in the same context. Because tariffs and quotas are similar in their market consequences and because together they are the core of trade protection by importers, we will examine the simple analytics of economic welfare changes when they are imposed. We also will consider briefly the maximum revenue tariff. Finally, we will sketch the outlines of the "optimal tariff" argument for a large trading economy.

TARIFFS

Fixed-Rate Tariff by Small Nation

Consider first the effects of a fixed-rate tariff applied by Nation A on the imports of the product q. The term "fixed-rate" means that the same import tax per unit is applied no matter how much is imported or what the international or domestic prices of the commodity are. For example, a fixed-rate tariff on a certain class of tobacco shipped into the United States might be, say, 20 cents per pound, irrespective of its market price or imported volume.

For the first analysis, consider a small nation whose imports of q, in the realistic range, cannot influence international prices. This situation is depicted in Fig. 5.1. As before, Fig. 5.1a reflects the domestic market and Fig. 5.1b the international market faced by this nation. The small-nation characteristic is reflected by the horizontal excess supply function for the rest of the world, $ES(R)$. Note that we measure imports toward the right from 0, in Fig. 5.1b.

If no tariffs or other trade distortions are applied by this nation in this market, the international and domestic prices are equal at p_1. Domestic producers supply an amount equivalent to ab, and bc is imported (Fig. 5.1a). This brings total consumption to ac. Fig. 5.1b shows imports of q equal to df. This is where Nation A's excess demand curve ED intersects $ES(R)$.

Now, for whatever reason, suppose the government decides to apply a fixed tariff to all imports of q. We show this by drawing ED^*, a vertical displacement of ED by the per unit amount of the tariff T. The function ED^* is the excess demand curve of this nation presented to the international market *after* the tariff is paid. It is a schedule of quantities demanded for import at various international prices considering the fact that a tariff must be paid. The intersection of ED^* (the tariff-burdened excess demand function) and $ES(R)$ establishes the new, smaller volume of imports. That decreased import volume causes *internal* prices to increase along the original ED function. (As a general practice in subsequent discussions we will use an asterisk (*) to denote a function displaced by a policy intervention. This intervention-caused displacement can occur either in the domestic market or the international sector.)

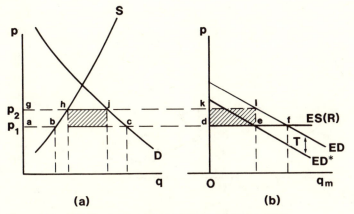

Figure 5.1 Effects of a fixed-rate tariff, small-nation case

Back to Fig. 5.1. The new international price of q is p_2. It is the world price p_1 plus the tariff T: $p_2 = p_1 + T$. The tariff makes imports of q more expensive than before. Domestic buyers in Nation A initially shun the now higher-priced imports, turning to domestic suppliers. Additional domestic supplies can be obtained only at higher prices along S. As prices for both imported and domestic goods increase, buyers reduce the use of both along D. The result is a new price equilibrium at p_2.

Because domestic supplies are expanding as domestic consumption dwindles, imports of q must fall. The new, smaller amount of imports is kl in Fig. 5.1b and hj in Fig. 5.1a. These imports bridge the narrowed gap between domestic production gh and domestic consumption gj at the higher price p_2 (Fig. 5.1a).

As long as imports are not snuffed out, tariff revenue is generated for the treasury. Its value is equal to the new import volume multiplied by T. This is the shaded area in Fig. 5.1a and Fig. 5.1b. The obvious economic consequences of this tariff other than revenue creation are a shrinkage of imports from df to de; a corresponding decrease in the total value of imports at the world price; an increase of domestic output from ab to gh; a fall in domestic consumption from ac to hj; and an increase in internal prices from p_1 to p_2. Exporters earn less gross revenue. Domestic sellers in Nation A earn more.

Whether or not domestic consumption expenditures are higher or lower with the tariff depends on the price elasticity e_D of the domestic demand function. If e_D is absolutely larger than -1.0, buyers spend less after the tariff. If e_D is absolutely less than -1.0, buyers spend more. In either case, they pay higher prices and purchase less q than they did without the tariff.

Large-Nation Tariff

Let us consider briefly the additional economic consequences that emerge if the nation levying a tariff bulks large in the international market for q. Figure

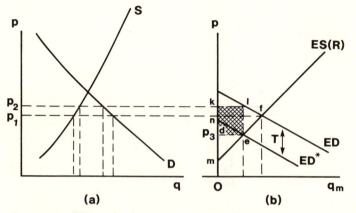

Figure 5.2 Effects of a fixed-rate tariff, large-nation case

5.2 shows such a case. It differs from the previous situation only because *ES(R)* is now positively sloped rather than horizontal in the relevant range. Hence, if Nation A increases its imports, world prices will rise. If it decreases its imports, world prices will fall.

In this case, the imposition of the tariff will have a price-increasing effect on the domestic market, as before. It also will have a depressing effect on world prices as the volume of imports into the nation shrinks from *nf* to *de*. This shrinkage of world trade volume will put downward pressure on world prices as supplies formerly destined for this nation are shifted elsewhere. In Fig. 5.2, this adjustment is indicated along *ES(R)*. The new equilibrium in the international market falls from that indicated at *f* to that indicated at *e* (Fig. 5.2*b*). The new domestic price is p_2 and the new world price is p_3. These two prices still differ from each other by *T* (the per-unit tariff value).

Because the world price falls, the domestic price increase caused by the tariff is less than if no change had occurred in the world price. The other impacts in the domestic market for *q* remain similar to those identified earlier. However, the tariff revenue is now *kled*. Importers still pay the tariff *T* as they bring *kl* units into the country, but the incidence of the tariff is shared by foreign sellers who receive lower prices and by domestic buyers who pay higher prices.

The price-changing incidence of the tariff need not be equally shared between the domestic and foreign markets. A close look at Fig. 5.2*b* reveals that the relative incidence of the tariff *T* depends on the relative absolute steepness (or price elasticity) of the *ED* and *ES(R)* functions. If both are the same in absolute slope (with *ED* negative and *ES(R)* positive), the tariff incidence will be split equally between domestic and foreign markets compared with the free trade position at *f*. If *ED* is absolutely steeper than *ES(R)*, the domestic price will rise more than the world price will fall as the tariff is imposed. On the other hand, if *ES(R)* is absolutely steeper than *ED*, the world price will fall more than the internal price will rise. These incidence effects are basically the same as with changing transfer costs between two trading nations, discussed in Chap. 4.

The United States, for example, is a very large importer of coffee, taking about 25 to 30 percent of annual world exports. If a sizable new tariff on coffee were imposed by the United States, world prices at New York would likely fall and internal prices would likely rise. The sum of the fall in world prices and the rise in domestic prices (both expressed at wholesale) would approximate the newly imposed tariff.

Tariffs imposed by large nations have relatively less protective consequences for domestic producers than identical tariffs imposed by small importers, other things being the same. This is because part of the internal price-raising impact of a large-nation tariff is dissipated in lower world prices. This effect prevents import volume from falling as much as if no international price decrease occurred. Since imports do not fall as much as in the small-nation case, tariff revenues for a fixed T are correspondingly higher in the large-nation case.

Tariffs so large that imports are entirely eliminated are called "prohibitive." In Fig. 5.1b, a tariff so high that ED^* intersects the vertical axis at or below point d would be prohibitive. Similarly, a tariff that pushed ED^* in Fig. 5.2 to a vertical intercept at or below point m would eliminate imports and thus be prohibitive.

Ad Valorem Tariff

The economic impacts and consequences of an ad valorem tariff are basically the same as with a fixed-rate tariff. The difference is in the tax levy itself. An ad valorem tariff usually is established as some percentage of the international price rather than a fixed per unit amount. Figure 5.3 shows how an ad valorem tariff displaces ED to ED^*. The function ED^* is the excess demand presented to the rest of the world in the presence of the ad valorem tariff. The vertical distance between ED and ED^* is the variable per unit value of the ad valorem tariff T. This value is larger at higher international prices and smaller at lower international prices, which are measured along ED^*. The intersection of ED^*

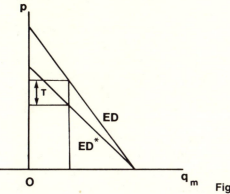

Figure 5.3 Ad valorem tariff

and the appropriate *ES(R)* establishes the international price against which the ad valorem tariff is calculated. Since *ED** lies below *ED* in both the fixed and ad valorem cases, the basic economic results are the same.

The ad valorem tariff is commonly stated as a percentage value—20 percent, 35 percent, etc.—of a readily observed international price. For example, assume that the world price of raw wool, expressed in pounds sterling, is £4.00 per kilogram and the ad valorem tariff into Great Britain is 20 percent. The tariff amount in this case is £0.80, and the internal price of cotton is £4.80 per kilogram. Should the international cotton price increase to £5.00, the tariff would increase to £1.00 per kilogram, lifting the internal price to £6.00.

QUOTAS

In the real world of international trade, tariffs have dwindled dramatically as a protective trade policy tool. Compared with the 1930s, tariffs around the trading world are becoming almost unimportant as barriers to commerce, especially for industrial products. With some exceptions, successive rounds of multilateral trade negotiations have been successful in reducing the average size and coverage of tariffs. However, ingenious nontariff barriers have been devised to achieve protection, especially in agricultural sectors.

Chief among these nontariff barriers are import quotas. While a tariff, fixed or ad valorem, directly creates a difference between international and domestic prices, the same two-price result is achieved indirectly by quantitative import restrictions. Let us look at the partial equilibrium economics of a simple import quota. Moreover, let us employ the large-nation assumption so that we can illustrate potential price effects on the international market.

A Binding Quota

An import quota enforced by the central authority has an effect on prices and trade only if it is "binding." A quota is binding when it restricts imports in a given period below the amount that otherwise would occur. Quotas are expressed as tons, bales, boxes, or pounds per year, month, or week. If the quota is larger than the volume that would be imported with free trade, it has no real effect. However, a binding quota will stint the domestic market of supplies. Prices will rise internally. Domestic producers will expand output and buyers will curtail purchases until the smaller excess demand is just balanced by the quota-determined volume of imports. In the large-nation case, the quota-induced stint of the domestic market implies a relative glut on the international market with price-depressing consequences. All of this is shown in Fig. 5.4.

The direct effect of a binding quota $\bar{q}_m$ is depicted in Fig. 5.4*b*. The original excess demand curve *ED* becomes *ED** with the intervention of a quota. At the quota amount, *ED** is completely vertical. At any international price below *d*, the amount $\bar{q}_m$ is imported. With this quota in place, the internal

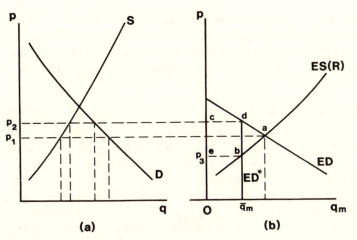

Figure 5.4   Effects of an import quota

price moves to p_2 and the world price falls to p_3, the latter being the international price at which *ES(R)* and *ED** intersect.

The overall consequences of a tariff and a quota are similar—internal prices rise, domestic production expands, domestic use declines, and world prices and imports fall. As with a tariff, the relative sizes of the domestic and international price changes depend on the absolute slopes (or price elasticities) of the excess supply and demand curves.

Quota Value

There is one important difference between a tariff and a quota. This involves the way in which a quota scheme is managed by the central authority. A market economy adapts to a consistently administered tariff more or less automatically. As prices change, output and expenditure allocations are adjusted and tax revenue flows into the treasury. However, in the case of a binding quota, the individual rights to import must be allocated in some fashion. Since these rights are scarce, they acquire value. In particular, the full per-unit value of these rights is the difference between the internal price p_2 at which imported goods are sold and the world price p_3 at which imported goods are purchased. This is shown as *db* in Fig. 5.4*b*.

Because this quota value is based solely on scarcity and not intrinsic value, it can be called economic "rent." These rents will exist as long as the overall quota is binding. The important distributional question is, who will capture them? In Fig. 5.4, the total value of quota rents is equal to area *cdbe*. If individual import quotas are distributed without charge on some basis (e.g., first-come, first-served, historical precedent, political expediency, at random), those who are fortunate enough to obtain a share in the overall quota will capture all rents available.

On the other hand, if quotas are auctioned to the highest bidders or sold at exactly the price *bd*, the government captures the rent and the outcome is exactly as if a tariff of *bd* had been levied. Of course, intermediate solutions are possible. They involve some distribution of the rent between the issuing government and the ultimate quota holders. A partial tax (or price) on quota allocations is one such possibility.

Government Importing Board

The partial equilibrium economics of an import quota as depicted in Fig. 5.4 also can be applied to the behavior of a government-authorized importing agency or board that has complete monopoly authority to import the product q. If the board decides to import $\bar{q}_m$ and no more, it can capture all the quota rent for itself. It will make its purchases on the international market at p_3, and make its domestic sales at p_2. As long as the board does not intervene further in the domestic market, it will capture the value shown as area *cdbe* in Fig. 5.4*b*.

WELFARE IMPLICATIONS OF TARIFFS AND QUOTAS

There are at least two ways to look at the economic effects of a protective trade policy in this partial equilibrium context. One is to study the direct effects on prices, production, trade, and consumption, then to identify the groups within the society who are likely to benefit or be hurt by the intervention. This is relatively straightforward, but occasionally ambiguous. Another way is to evaluate the economic welfare changes that occur. Following this latter path requires some understanding of the concepts of consumer and producer surplus. In this section we will use both approaches with the understanding that the second approach may transcend the analytical background of some readers. However, the summary passage at the end of the section will capture the basic conclusions.

Gainers and Losers

The imposition of a tariff or an import quota will benefit some individuals and impose costs on others. These effects can be seen readily in Figs. 5.1 and 5.3. Imagine that we are considering the effects of a tariff or quota on participants in the beef market. In the first instance, a tariff or quota will benefit domestic cattle producers who obtain higher prices for more output behind the import barrier. By extension, we can argue that individuals and firms who supply productive inputs like feed and veterinary service to the protected producers will benefit because of additional demand for their products and services. Similarly, an increase in beef prices will spill over into the markets for related products like pork, lamb, poultry, and perhaps dairy products. Prices in these markets will tend to be stronger as beef prices move higher.

Domestic consumers of beef, either locally produced or imported, will be hurt as will buyers of closely related products. They will face higher prices and, consequently, will buy less. Because import volume tends to shrink behind a tariff or a binding quota, it follows that individuals and firms who handle imported beef will lose markets and earnings. With a tariff on beef imports, the government treasury will benefit through additional revenue. However, the costs of administration and tariff collection have not been reflected in our simple graphics. They might be substantial.

When considering a binding beef-import quota, we would need to know how the allocation is handled. A free allocation will benefit those who somehow obtain the scarce import rights. They will capture all the quota rents. An auction, sale, or taxation of individual quota rights will capture at least some rent for the issuing agency, diminishing that obtained by the quota holders. In summary, the domestic gainers from a beef import restraint are cattle producers, those who supply them with inputs, producers of related products, and the government treasury or the import quota holders. The losers are consumers and, by extension, firms that handle and merchandise imports.

Though foreign suppliers are not a central topic in this analysis, we can be confident that foreign suppliers to the tariff- or quota-burdened market will lose. In the small-import-nation case, they will lose import volume only. In the large-nation case, they will both lose import volume and feel downward price pressure on all sales tied to international prices. Possible foreign gainers are consumers in nations where downward price pressure occurs because of the smaller volume of trade caused by the tariff or quota.

Although we can identify with fair certainty who gains and who loses, the relative sizes of these gains and losses and their distribution across an economy are by no means clear from this reasoning. Some additional ideas are needed. This is where producer and consumer surplus comes in.

Welfare Analysis of Tariffs and Quotas

Consumer surplus is fundamentally the net value that consumers as a group obtain by being able to purchase as much as they wish at the going market price rather than having to pay, successively, the highest price they would be prepared to offer for each additional unit. For instance, no consumer surplus for beef would occur if each buyer had to negotiate individually with a clever monopolist for every unit purchased. Such a monopolist could extract the highest price each buyer would be willing to pay for each successive unit of beef. The simplest partial equilibrium expression of consumer surplus for a product is usually taken as the area under the relevant demand curve and above the going price.

A price change will change consumer surplus. In going from p_1 to p_2 in Fig. 5.5, consumer surplus falls by the combined area $A + B + C + D$. This is the change in the area under the demand curve above the market price.

Producer surplus is fundamentally the net value obtained by owners of productive assets fixed (at least momentarily) in the sector to be analyzed. It

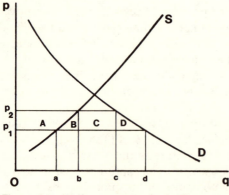

Figure 5.5   Welfare aspects of a tariff or quota

is the gross return to those assets after fully variable costs are accounted for. These assets could be land, buildings, equipment, or specialized human skills. Like consumer surplus, producer surplus is a slippery concept, but as an abstract tool of reasoning it can be useful. With the assumption that the aggregate supply curve for the product in question reflects the marginal cost of additional output, producer surplus is the area above the relevant supply curve but below the price received for output. This is so because the area under the marginal cost (supply) function represents payments to variable factors of production. Thus, the area above is the total return to all fixed factors. The partial equilibrium view of the increase in producer surplus caused by a price change from p_1 to p_2 can be identified in Fig. 5.5 as area A, the change in the area above the supply curve and below the market price.

With these ideas of producer and consumer surplus in hand, a somewhat closer analysis of tariffs and quotas can be developed. Assume that the free trade position in the q market is associated with p_1 in Fig. 5.5. In this case, $0a$ is produced domestically, ad is imported, and the total $0d$ is consumed. A tariff or a quota is introduced that raises the internal price to p_2, at which $0b$ is produced, bc is imported, and $0c$ is consumed.

This policy-induced change lowers consumer surplus from the free trade position by the amount $A + B + C + D$. This is the partial equilibrium economic cost of this change to consumers. Can we trace its distribution through the economy? Some of it, area A, is picked up as an increase in producer surplus. This value goes to owners of fixed assets that produce q. Some of it, area C, goes either to the government as tariff revenue or to import quota holders as economic rent.

Some of the value lost by consumers goes to sellers of variable inputs. This is area B. It measures the *additional* payments to variable inputs needed to attract them away from other uses into the q sector so that domestic output can expand from $0a$ to $0b$. Since resources attracted into the q industry are not available for other use, the area B reflects part of the marginal value of output not produced elsewhere in the economy because of the expansion of q. Economists usually consider this area B to be an "efficiency" loss to the economy. This is because some production elsewhere in the economy is sacrificed to produce more q at p_2. This additional q, measured by ab in Fig. 5.5, could always be obtained via free trade at p_1.

This leaves area D to be explained. No one in the society picks up area D in redistribution. It is a "deadweight" consumption loss because consumers allocate expenditures away from the now more expensive q to other things. It is generally speaking part of the real income lost by consumers because of the price increase from p_1 to p_2, with no compensating changes occurring in other prices or in money incomes. Unlike areas A, B, and C, it cannot be traced elsewhere in the economy. It just vanishes.

This welfare analysis, abstract though it is, indicates that aside from the redistribution of A and C away from consumers to others, net losses occur in the economy. They are efficiency losses in production (B) and deadweight consumption losses (D). One can view these losses as the implicit price an economy pays for (1) the privilege of protecting the producers of q with a tariff or a quota and (2) the accumulation of tariff revenues or quota rents. Their relative sizes in any actual case depend on the magnitude of the induced price change and the price elasticities of supply and demand. The actual values may be large or small, known or unknown, but as long as p_2 is higher than p_1, these net welfare losses (sometimes called "social losses") will exist. In addition, the society imposing tariffs or quotas also must be prepared to accept the internal redistribution of economic values that occurs.

Consider again our beef import-tariff example. The consumers of beef lose economic value as internal prices, burdened by the new tariff, increase from previous levels. Part of this value is a redistribution to cattle growers and shows up as additional profits (or net returns) to beef production. Part of the lost consumer value for beef is transferred to the government treasury as tariff revenue.

As beef production expands behind the tariff, additional land, feed grains, labor, veterinary services, etc., are drawn into the cattle industry at the expense of other livestock and, possibly, crop enterprises. Part of the output value of these other commodities that are sacrificed to expand beef production is lost to the society as an efficiency loss. The remaining amount of surplus value lost by beef consumers simply vanishes as a deadweight loss as consumers' real income falls.

SELECTING A TARIFF RATE

It is probably true that existing tariff rates around the world are more or less arbitrary values. They are the net result of factors such as political compromise, historical accident, and complex international negotiation. The same is true for import quotas. However, it is possible to illustrate some abstract principles of tariff setting to which any current practice could be compared. We will discuss two such principles here—maximum revenue tariffs and "optimal" tariffs. These principles can also be adapted to the tariff equivalent values of import quotas and quota rents. Similarly, entirely symmetric arguments can be developed for the setting of export taxes, as discussed in Chap. 12.

Maximum Revenue Tariff

Suppose that Nation A wishes to set a tariff on imported tea. This duty will protect domestic tea growers as an incidental feature, but its main purpose will be to generate revenue for the government. How should it proceed? Fig. 5.6 illustrates this question. Fig. 5.6a is the usual excess supply and demand picture, with the free trade import volume indicated by $\bar{q}$. Fig. 5.6b measures imports on the horizontal axis and tariff revenue (the tariff rate times import volume) on the vertical axis.

When free trade prevails, the tariff rate is zero. Hence, no tariff revenue is generated at $\bar{q}$. If the tariff rate is greater than $a - b$ in Fig. 5.6a, it is prohibitive and no imports will occur. Again, the tariff revenue is zero at point 0. In between these extremes, some tariff revenue is generated. The general result

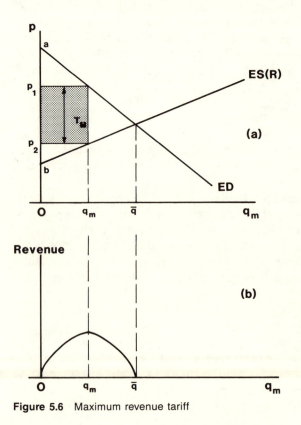

Figure 5.6 Maximum revenue tariff

is that revenue will rise and then fall as tariffs increase and imports dwindle. The place at which revenue peaks, between 0 and $\bar{q}$, is import volume associated with the maximum revenue tariff—shown as q_M in Fig. 5.6. The revenue-maximizing tariff is T_M, as indicated in Fig. 5.6b. The internal price is then p_2 and the world price is p_1. The exact position of q_M and the exact value of T_M naturally depend on the position and shape of the ED and $ES(R)$ functions. If, for instance, both are straight lines, it can be shown that q_M is one-half the distance between 0 and $\bar{q}$.

Other shapes for ED and $ES(R)$ will yield other results, but there is always a maximum revenue tariff position somewhere between 0 and $\bar{q}$. In the small-nation case, for instance, the maximum revenue tariff occurs when the ratio of the domestic price to the tariff is exactly equal to the absolute value of the price elasticity of the importing country's excess demand function.

Optimal Tariff Policy

There is another line of reasoning in trade policy economics that shows that the welfare analysis discussed earlier in this chapter is not necessarily the last word on welfare gains and losses from protective trade policy, even within the partial equilibrium context. The basic idea behind this argument is that a large importing nation can exploit its international market power via tariffs or import controls to offset (or more than offset) the combined deadweight and efficiency losses caused domestically. As it faces the rest of the trading world, a large trading nation can select an optimal tariff for its own benefit.

Consider Fig. 5.7, in which a large importing nation exhibits an excess demand function for imports of ED and faces a positively sloping excess supply function from the rest of the world, $ES(R)$. Point e is the initial, free trade equilibrium. Imagine that a tariff of $a - f$ is levied, generating the ED^* function shown in Fig. 5.7. The new international equilibrium is at g, and tariff revenues of $abgf$ are generated as domestic prices rise, world prices fall, and imports decline.

A little study and experimentation with Figs. 5.2 or 5.4 can convince one that the shaded area bde in Fig. 5.7 is the sum of the tariff-induced domestic production efficiency and deadweight consumer losses—areas B and D in Fig. 5.5. Furthermore, the area $abdc$ in Fig. 5.7 is equivalent to area C in Fig. 4.5. (Recall that C is the value of the consumer surplus loss redistributed to the government as tariff revenue.)

It is possible that the *additional* tariff revenue generated by pressing down the world price, area $cdgf$, can be made large enough to offset the welfare losses measured by bde. Figure 5.7 is drawn to suggest this. Hence the government, in principle, could use the funds from area $cdgf$ to compensate for the net social losses measured by bde and perhaps have something left over. The more inelastic $ES(R)$ is relative to the absolute price elasticity of ED, the more likely it is that such an optimal tariff policy can be pursued successfully. If the $ES(R)$ function is completely elastic, as with the small-nation assumption, the world

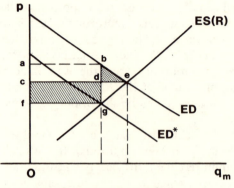

Figure 5.7   Optimal tariff selection

price cannot be pressed down by the importing country. Then the optimal tariff is zero.

The complete theory of the optimal tariff for a large nation includes rules for setting this tariff rate to maximize the difference between tariff revenues generated and the social losses caused by the tariff's adoption. No account is taken explicitly in this theory of the gains and losses sustained by foreigners as a result of the tariff. An elaboration of these topics would carry us beyond the scope of this book. However, the maximum revenue tariff and the optimal tariff are not the same. It is generally true that the optimal tariff rate is smaller than the maximum revenue tariff rate. Hence, an optimal tariff will reduce imports less than a revenue-maximizing tariff.

SUMMARY

By raising the domestic price of both imported and similar local goods, tariffs and quotas punish consumers. Tariffs act to raise internal prices and, as a result, push imports down from their nontariff volume. Quotas reduce imports directly and, as a result, stint the domestic market, causing internal prices to rise above nonquota values. The losses sustained by consumers are partially offset by gains to owners of domestic production facilities who earn higher, protected prices and expand their output. Also, gains are achieved by the government treasury with tariffs or by those who capture rent on the allocation of scarce import quotas.

In total, these sources of gain do not offset the consumers' loss. Part of this net social loss is an efficiency loss, sustained as the economy produces protected output that could otherwise be obtained on the world market at lower cost. The rest of the net social loss is called a deadweight consumer loss because of necessary consumption adjustments caused by the uncompensated price increase of the protected items.

It is possible that a large importing nation can offset part or all of these net social losses by exploiting its international market power. By driving down world prices with a tariff, the net domestic social losses can be offset by tariff revenues attributable to the decrease in world prices. The domestic social losses will still occur. Whether or not they can be offset is problematical and depends on the nation's role in the relevant international market. Maximum revenue tariffs are generally higher than the analytically more-complex optimal tariffs.

QUESTIONS

5.1 Illustrate and explain why a binding import quota on tea will insulate internal tea prices in the nation of Dorway from fluctuation caused by world market instability.

5.2 Assume that Dorway increases its annual tea import quota by 15 percent. Illustrate and discuss the welfare implications of this maneuver from the viewpoint of Dorwegian society.

5.3 To protect its domestic potato industry, the nation of Lower Magnolia has enacted a "tariff-quota." This involves a low tariff on imports if the import volume (per month) is below a fixed quota amount. However, if monthly potato imports exceed this amount, a higher tariff rate applies. Discuss and illustrate the economics of this trade policy. How would this scheme affect price fluctuations inside Lower Magnolia caused by seasonally changing excess supplies from the rest of the world?

5.4 Magnifica is a major importer of natural rubber from the international market. It has been protecting its synthetic rubber manufacturers by means of an annual, binding import quota. Individual shares of this quota are allocated to various importing firms based on historical precedent. The Magnifican government has decided to replace the quota with a tariff, but it is trying to decide whether a fixed or ad valorem tariff should be used. The new tariff will ensure the same internal protection for the synthetic rubber sector as last year. Describe the economic implications of moving from a quota to a tariff. Also outline the differences to be expected in price and import behavior depending on the kind of tariff selected as world rubber supplies fluctuate.

ADDITIONAL READINGS

Corden, W. M. 1971. *The Theory of Protection*, Clarendon Press, Oxford, England. (The partial equilibrium economics of tariffs and quotas—a bit more advanced than this book.)

Enke, S. 1944. The monopsony case for tariffs, *Quarterly Journal of Economics*, 58:229–245. (An early and quite clear exposition of the partial equilibrium basics of the optimal tariff argument.)

Grennes, T. 1984. *International Economics*, Prentice-Hall, Englewood Cliffs, New Jersey, Chaps. 7 and 8. (A broad, clear textbook presentation of tariff and quota economics, mainly the partial equilibrium approach.)

Hillman, J. 1978. *Non-tariff Agricultural Trade Barriers*, University of Nebraska Press,

Lincoln, Nebraska, Chap. 5. (A largely nontechnical discussion of real-world quotas in agricultural trade.)

Institute for Contemporary Studies. 1979. *Tariffs, Quotas, and Trade: The Politics of Protectionism*, Institute for Contemporary Studies, San Francisco, California. (A collection of essays mainly by economists on trade and protectionism issues.)

Salvatore, D. 1983. *International Economics*, Schaum's Outline Series in Economics, McGraw-Hill Book Co., New York, New York, Chap. 6. (A graphical blend of general and partial equilibrium tariff analysis, with numerous examples and problems.)

Chapter 6

Price Guarantees with Variable Levies or Deficiency Payments

Agricultural price and income policies in many countries and for many commodities hinge on some form of farm price guarantees. These guarantees are often higher than free markets will deliver. Consequently, some central intervention must occur to tip the operation of the market or loosen the government purse in favor of the protected producers. When international trade in protected products is important, even potentially, the intervention mechanism must include trade policy dimensions.

To protect internal price guarantees, tariffs and quotas have operational drawbacks. Fixed or ad valorem tariffs allow fluctuations in world prices to be transmitted fully or partly into the domestic market. Import quotas, if binding, insulate the domestic market from world price changes, but they may amplify domestic price swings caused by internal demand and supply fluctuations. Downward domestic price fluctuations from whatever source usually undermine protective policies.

A number of policy schemes have been devised over the years by nations to overcome these shortcomings of traditional tariffs and quotas. Two prominent examples for import products are variable import levies and deficiency payments. Their primary function is to protect a domestic producer price guarantee from being undermined or overwhelmed by the behavior of international markets. However, they differ substantially from each other in operational details and in broad economic effects beyond the immediate aims of producer protection.

VARIABLE LEVIES

As a protective trade policy, variable import levies are among the most effective, hence notorious, in the international arena. When combined with price guarantees to domestic producers, variable levies (sometimes called "minimum import price schemes") provide solid price protection to sectors politically powerful enough to press their claims effectively. Price guarantees and variable levies are at the heart of the Common Agricultural Policy of the European Economic Community and other European countries. Similar schemes are also employed elsewhere in the trading world for both agricultural and industrial products.

In actual practice, policies like tariffs and quotas can be bewilderingly complex. Our purpose in this section is not to unravel the confusing lexicon and intricacies of various ongoing programs but to examine the relatively simple, direct economic effects of variable levies. Simply put, variable levies are employed to protect domestic price guarantees from being defeated by trade flows. Hence, the starting point for us is to assume that price guarantees, affecting both producers and consumers, are established. The process of establishment and subsequent adjustment need not overly concern us here. It could be purely political or it could be based on mathematical formulas, historical precedent, or some combination of them.

With price guarantees in place, an administrative mechanism is needed to calculate and impose import tariffs that exactly bridge the difference between the higher price guarantee and the relevant, lower international price. This mechanism must be sufficiently flexible so that import levies can be continually recalculated and adjusted to account for short-term changes in world prices. (For instance, the European Economic Community adjusts some of its variable import levies on a daily basis.) Once in operation, the variable levy effectively disconnects domestic prices of affected imports from international prices. Furthermore, it transfers domestic demand or supply instability to the world market via changes in imports. In addition, revenues may be generated for the central authority just as with fixed or ad valorem tariffs.

Suppose that on a particular business day the internal price guarantee for a specific grade of barley in the European Economic Community is the equivalent of $150 per tonne. If the relevant international price at, say, Rotterdam is $115 per tonne, the variable levy (simply speaking) charged by the EEC Commission to all would-be barley importers is $35 per tonne. Should the next day's international price drop by $5 to $100 per tonne, the levy will increase by an equal amount to $40 per tonne, keeping the internal price at $150 per tonne. Although the complexities of the real markets and the Common Agriculture Policy make this illustration very rudimentary, it does capture the basic workings of the scheme.

Economic Effects

A partial equilibrium view of a basic variable import levy scheme is presented in Fig. 6.1 for Nation A, a small importer. In Fig. 6.1a, p_s indicates the price guarantee to be pursued. If no protective trade policy were employed, this price guarantee could not be achieved inside Nation A since world prices, hence internal prices, would fluctuate between p_1 and p_2 in this illustration as $ES(R)$ moved up and down between $ES(R)_1$ and $ES(R)_2$ (Fig. 6.1b).

The establishment of a variable levy scheme to secure p_s inside Nation A produces the adjusted excess demand curve ED^*, which is the original ED curve from point f down to point a, and then a perfectly vertical segment at all lower international prices. The portions of the domestic supply and demand functions below p_s are not relevant for market operation.

The price guarantee p_s is assured because the levy is equal to ab when p_1 prevails on the international market and equal to ac when p_2 prevails. As world prices fall, the per-unit levy increases. As prices rise, the levy decreases. Inside Nation A, the guarantee p_s is maintained. The levy fund is collected by the central authority of A. At p_1, the levy fund generates total revenues of *dabe*. As long as internal conditions remain constant, imports will hold at $eb = da$ units.

If world prices should move above d, the variable levy scheme would cease to operate because open market prices without protection would be above p_s. Import volume would decrease. However, as long as world prices are below d, variable levies sustain the support rate and enrich the treasury. If p_s were to be a maximum as well as a minimum price guarantee, some form of import subsidy would be required as long as there is some volume of excess demand at p_s. We will encounter the economics of import subsidies in Chap. 9.

While a variable levy is in operation, any fluctuations or trends in the relative positions of D and S in the domestic market will not depress the domestic price below p_s. All adjustments will occur as fluctuations in the

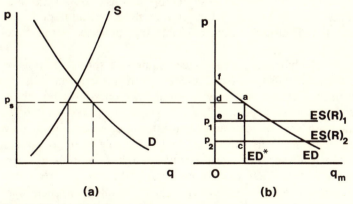

Figure 6.1 Variable levy scheme

amount imported and available for consumption. Figure 6.2 illustrates how a shift in domestic supply from S to S' changes the adjusted excess demand curve from ED^* to $ED^{*'}$. As domestic production at p_2 increases by ab units of volume in Fig. 6.2a, imports decrease by an equal amount—namely, ef in Fig. 6.2b. Domestic consumption remains constant, indicated by point c along D in Fig. 6.2a.

Gains and Losses

The gains, losses, and economic welfare effects of the variable import levy scheme are directly comparable to those with ordinary tariffs or quotas, discussed in Chap. 5 and illustrated in Fig. 5.5. Both efficiency and consumer deadweight losses occur in the domestic economy as producers enjoy the protection afforded by p_s and the adjustable levies. Because the variable levy intervention occurs at the point of importation, consumer prices inside the nation also reflect the price guarantee. Hence, consumer surplus losses occur just as they do with ordinary tariffs or quotas.

For a large importer facing a positively sloped $ES(R)$ function, it is possible that p_s can be set high enough so that, depending on the price elasticity of $ES(R)$ relative to ED, the variable levy fund could generate sufficient extra revenue to offset the social losses caused by elevating p_s above the free trade level. This argument follows exactly the same line of reasoning as the optimal tariff discussion in Chap. 5. Instead of setting the tariff and allowing the internal and world prices to adjust, this approach sets the internal price and allows the world price and the levy to adjust. The analytical results are the same.

The Variable Levy as a Protective Policy

Using the variable levy scheme to secure internal price guarantees is effective and relatively easy, once it is in place. Because it disconnects world prices from the domestic market, it introduces price stability to internal markets. However, this price stability may be associated with increased potential for farm income instability to occur as domestic supplies fluctuate from season to season. With no mitigating upward price movements in short crop seasons or downward fluctuations in bumper years, producer returns in a large importing nation may swing more widely than if farm prices were flexible and connected to the world market.

A variable levy mechanism, once in place, requires no special analysis or expertise to operate, and tends to generate revenue for the government treasury. Because it does all these things, it is very unpopular with nations who export the products to which it is applied.

The insulated price guarantees tend to shrink imports below what they otherwise would be in the short run. Over time, the stable price guarantees may induce the domestic supply curve to shift to the right faster than it otherwise would, as in Fig. 6.2. These tendencies are disturbing to exporting nations. Moreover, import nations typically view their variable levy schemes as

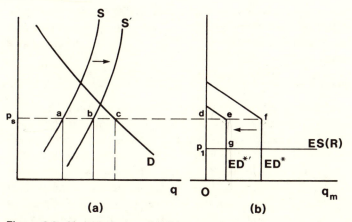

Figure 6.2 Variable levy and shifting supply

nonnegotiable in international forums. Ordinary tariffs and quotas affect trade directly. They can be raised, lowered, or changed in negotiations. Variable levies are really a process, not a specific entity. They are an adjunct to domestic price guarantees. Thus, to negotiate a variable levy with one or more trading partners is to allow external influence into decisions about the level and process of establishing p_s. The users of variable levies are hardly ever willing to do this.

DEFICIENCY PAYMENTS

Producer protection by means of import tariffs, quotas, or variable levies requires that domestic consumers or buyers pay prices for protected goods that are higher than otherwise. In fact, the loss of consumer surplus domestically because of the higher, protected prices is the source of value gains by producers, quota holders, and the national treasury. However, there are policy mechanisms that sidestep some or all of the direct loss to consumers even as protection from foreign competition is pursued on behalf of producers. A leading example in this category is production subsidy by means of deficiency payments.

This particular policy scheme involves direct payments by taxpayers rather than transfers from consumers. The shift in the burden from consumers to taxpayers occurs because consumers are permitted to purchase both imports and competitive domestic output at open market prices. The structure of official price guarantees to domestic farmers is supported by direct payments from the treasury to producers. No tariffs, quotas, or levies are required. Hence, trade is not directly restricted.

To illustrate, suppose the guaranteed producer price of cotton in Nation A is the equivalent of $1.70 per kilogram in the bale, and the open market price is $1.35. In this case, cotton producers would receive a deficiency payment of $0.35 per kilogram of cotton sold. If market prices increased to $1.45

per kilogram, the deficiency payment would drop to $0.25 per kilogram. These payments presumably would be made through a government agency of Nation A responsible for managing the program. No other direct market or trade intervention would occur.

Analytical Framework

Let us look at a simple partial equilibrium approach to this program. Consider the now-familiar, demand-supply framework in Fig. 6.3 for the small-nation case. Here, p_1 is the international price in the absence of any protection. Both domestic producers and buyers respond to p_1. In this free trade situation, quantity ac in Fig. 6.3b would be imported. This is also equal to quantity de in Fig. 6.3a. Now suppose that the government decides to set p_s as the guaranteed per-unit price to producers. Instead of intervening directly in the market to ensure that producers receive p_s, the government elects to rely on deficiency payments. How would this scheme operate?

Producers would be guaranteed p_s, but not all of that per-unit value necessarily would come from the marketplace. Market prices would be allowed to seek a level consistent with the unfettered flow of imports. The difference, if any, between the price guarantee p_s and the market price p_1 is covered by direct payments from the government to producers. In Fig. 6.3, the price guarantee causes domestic output to expand by fg units above free market production. The deficiency payment is $p_s - p_1$ per unit on all units produced and sold. Its total value is indicated by the shaded area in Fig. 6.3a. The higher p_s is relative to p_1, the larger the deficiency payments are both in their per-unit value and as total government outlay.

Buyers in the domestic market still face p_1. Thus, no negative consumption effect occurs. If this producer price guarantee were sustained by a variable

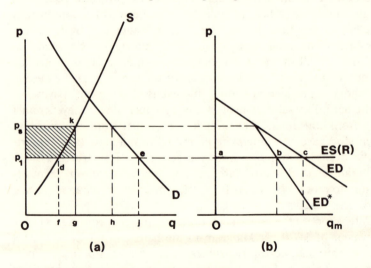

(a)   (b)

Figure 6.3 Deficiency payments and imports

levy or a specific tariff, for example, prices to buyers would be p_s and consumption would fall by hj units. But with deficiency payments, consumption stays at $0j$. However, because domestic production expands by fg units, imports must drop by an equal amount. (As usual, we assume that domestic and imported items are fully substitutable for each other.)

In Fig. 6.3b, we can see how this deficiency payments scheme indirectly alters the original ED function. Because p_s is guaranteed to domestic producers, international and domestic prices for this commodity can change drastically without any direct impact on domestic output. This is true as long as open market prices are below p_s. The new excess demand function, reflecting the internal deficiency payments scheme, is ED^*. It is the horizontal distance between D and the vertical line kg in Fig. 6.3a. The new ED^* measures the amount of imports demanded at various market prices when p_s is guaranteed to domestic producers. The slope of ED^* is exactly the same as the slope of D because the only adjustment in import volume occurring at various market prices is because domestic quantities demanded change. Thus, the horizontal difference between ED and ED^* in Fig. 6.3b at prices below p_s is equal to the horizontal difference between S and the vertical line segment kg in Fig. 6.3a. This difference at any market price is the additional production caused by the higher price guarantee relative to that market price.

If $ES(R)$ and the world price dropped below p_1 in this illustration, imports and consumption would expand along ED^* and D, respectively. Domestic producers would notice no change in their guaranteed price, only a fall in the portion obtained via the market and an increase in the amount provided by deficiency payments. As the per-unit deficiency payment grew, the total government outlays would increase. Consumers would benefit, but as taxpayers they would shoulder the additional financial burden for this price guarantee program.

Gainers and Losers

Deficiency payments as a protection device leave consumers, strictly as consumers, in an unchanged welfare position compared with no program. Domestic producers obviously are benefited by the price guarantees. They achieve protection at the direct expense of taxpayers and the government.

To foreign suppliers, deficiency payments are a less onerous method of protection than measures that raise and insulate internal consumers from the international market. This is because the import volume is restricted less stringently than with equally protective tariffs, quotas, or variable levies.

Recall the welfare analysis illustrated in Fig. 5.5. The deficiency payments scheme we are now discussing generates the production efficiency loss of area B in that figure. This area measures the net value of goods and services sacrificed by the domestic economy to produce the additional units of q at the guaranteed price. An area corresponding to A in Fig. 5.5 for the deficiency payments case reflects a transfer of value from taxpayers to domestic producers. Together, areas A and B comprise the deficiency payments transfer.

Although there is a production efficiency loss, no deadweight consumer loss occurs with deficiency payments as it does with tariffs and quotas. Therefore, the net social loss experienced by the society is less with deficiency payments than with tariffs, quotas, variable levies, or other devices that elevate consumer prices as a consequence of their operation. This general conclusion emerges from the study of virtually any type of production subsidy. In particular, the deficiency payments approach described here is in fact an open-ended production subsidy that ensures p_s to producers without directly altering the market price.

From the protected sector's viewpoint, a deficiency payments scheme may have one or two strategic drawbacks. Most important is that the full amount of protection given to this industry will appear clearly in the national budget and in the records of the operating agency. This transfer, therefore, is subject to direct scrutiny by taxpayers and their political representatives. None of the protective transfer is hidden in higher consumer prices, and no tariff revenues are obtained. Consequently, it is likely that domestic producers will be forced to restate and defend their favored status each time budget allocations are made or each time market prices drop noticeably. While this reexamination is healthy for the economy as a whole, it is not an experience that highly protected producer groups relish.

Some producers' representatives may argue that their constituents do not like to receive part of their incomes *directly* as a subsidy, preferring rather to "earn" them in the market. This may be true in individual cases, but such an attitude, if it is widespread, can affect the enthusiasm with which protection-seeking producers support deficiency payments as opposed to other schemes.

Large-Nation Case

We will not discuss in detail how the large-nation case affects the deficiency payments approach. The economics is straightforward. Look again at Fig. 6.3 and imagine a positively sloped *ES(R)* function in Fig. 6.3*b* passing through point *c*. Clearly, the intersection of this *ES(R)* curve with *ED** will produce a world price lower than p_1. This occurs because imports in the presence of a deficiency payments policy are smaller than they would otherwise be.

Consumers in the domestic economy will experience prices below p_1. They will demand more *q*. All of this additional volume will come from lower-priced imports. Thus the deficiency payments scheme, while redistributing income toward producers, can make consumers better off than with free trade if the protected increase in domestic production at p_s causes world prices to fall. However, as the international price falls, carrying the domestic market price with it, the deficiency payments burden on the taxpayers increases—the shaded area in Fig. 6.3*a* will expand.

Production Control

The simplest application of a deficiency payments scheme involves no constraints on the amount of domestic production eligible for payments. It is an open-ended production subsidy. Yet with high prices guaranteed for domestic output and direct budget scrutiny almost inevitable, it is clearly possible that some upper limit on total payment outlays might be imposed by government authorities seeking to reduce or retard expansion in treasury costs.

Although domestic authorities will not be able to do much, if anything, about world prices, they can influence the total budget for deficiency payments, even if p_s is maintained. One way to do this is to control production by some means. This involves keeping S from moving to the right as fast as it otherwise might, or even inducing it to move to the left. In agriculture, production controls are achieved by such measures as reducing the land area devoted to protected crops, invoking production (or marketing) quotas on producers or, in the case of livestock, promoting the reduction of producing or breeding herds and flocks.

It is also possible for the government to set a maximum (or base) amount of output on which deficiency payments can be collected. The apportioning of this total amount to individual producers and the pricing of production beyond the official base are closely related to the management problems associated with multiple price or market discrimination schemes, discussed in Chap. 11.

SUMMARY

The variable import levy as a protective device overcomes some operational shortcomings of both tariffs and quotas. It detaches domestic prices completely from the world market and tends to promote internal price, if not income, stability for the affected producers. The operation of a variable levy scheme allows the protecting import nation to follow an internal price guarantee system without external market interference. It also generates revenue for the central treasury. As a protective device, the variable import levy is among the most effective, hence notorious, in the international arena.

A simple deficiency payment scheme shifts the protective burden entirely away from consumers to taxpayers. In this particular case, the production subsidy, relative to the international price, is provided by direct government payments to producers. These payments bridge the gap between the guaranteed prices and open market prices. Social losses with deficiency payments are smaller than those associated with tariffs, quotas, or variable levies for the same level of producer protection.

QUESTIONS

6.1 The nation of Equinox applies variable import levies to protect a high guaranteed internal price for meat and livestock. The two major meat exporters, Beafland and Porcina, cooperate with each other to capture the variable levy revenue that otherwise would flow into the Equinox federal treasury. Illustrate and explain how this could occur.

6.2   Equinox also applies variable levies against imports of potatoes. Show how and why price fluctuations on the world's unstable potato market are prevented from affecting Equinox's internal market.

6.3   The country of Niceland traditionally has protected its coffee growers by means of a high guaranteed price and variable import levies. The Nicelandic government is considering moving to a deficiency payments scheme to achieve the same level of producer protection. Analyze the economic effects of this proposal, including its basic welfare implications.

6.4   The small island country of New Dealand has decided as a matter of national security to become self-sufficient in the production of its staple food grain, wheat. Wheat is now imported in relatively small amounts. The debate is whether to achieve this objective by means of deficiency payments or an appropriate tariff. You are asked to advise the government on this matter. Outline your advice and the reasoning behind it.

ADDITIONAL READINGS

Agricultural Extension Service, University of Minnesota, St. Paul, Minnesota. 1978. *Speaking of Trade: Its Effect on Agriculture*, Special Report No. 72, Chap. 3. (A partial equilibrium presentation of deficiency payments and variable levies.)

Cohen, M. H. 1982. Sweden's Agricultural Policy, Foreign Agricultural Economic Report 175, Economic Research Service, U.S. Department of Agriculture, Washington, D.C. (Especially pages 14–23. Includes a good, clear nontechnical discussion of variable levies outside the usual European Economic Community context.)

Grennes, T. 1984. *International Economics*, Prentice-Hall, Englewood Cliffs, New Jersey, pp. 198–200. (Short partial equilibrium presentations of variable levies.)

McCalla, A. F., and Josling, T. E. 1981. *Imperfect Markets in Agricultural Trade*, Allanheld, Osmun & Co., Montclair, New Jersey, Chap. 4. (A discussion of domestic agricultural price policies and their interaction through trade, including deficiency payments and variable levies.)

Sorenson, V. L. 1975. *International Trade Policy: Agriculture and Development*, International and Business Studies, Michigan State University, East Lansing, Michigan, pp. 77–84. (A partial equilibrium comparison of various forms of protection, including deficiency payments and variable levies.)

Chapter 7

Proportional Import Quotas and Direct Production Subsidies

This chapter deals with two further protective devices that benefit domestic agricultural producers who compete with imports. They are proportional import quotas and direct production subsidies. Each displays economic elements that blend the effects of tariffs and quotas on the one hand and deficiency payments on the other. We link them together in this chapter because they provide domestic producers a measure of price and income protection but do not typically involve the establishment of specific internal price guarantees.

PROPORTIONAL IMPORT QUOTAS

Proportional import quotas are sometimes called "mixing" regulations, sometimes "domestic content" regulations. From the consumer's viewpoint, they are more onerous than deficiency payments for achieving a given amount of producer protection but less so than a tariff. On the other hand, they are less onerous for taxpayers since no direct treasury costs are required. The fundamental goal of import regulation by means of proportional quotas is to hold imports down to a maximum percentage share of the total domestic market.

The term "mixing regulation" is most often used with agricultural commodities or other relatively homogeneous raw materials. Flour sold on the domestic market of Nation A, for example, may be required to contain a minimum of 35 percent domestically grown wheat. Cigarettes produced domestically in Nation B may be allowed to contain no more than 50 percent of imported leaf. Where physical blending of this kind is not feasible, a mixing regulation might take the form of a "quantity link." That is, import licenses for foreign-made clothing or textiles might be issued in Nation C in fixed proportion to the production and sale of similar domestic articles. For instance, an import license for a certain quality of foreign sweaters might be issued to a clothing merchant in Nation C only after the applicant presented evidence of the purchase of, say, twice as many domestically made sweaters.

Domestic content regulations are the industrial counterpart of mixing regulations for agricultural commodities and raw materials. They are relatively common in the protection of automotive manufacturing industries. Such regulations require that some minimum proportion of the final value of all automobiles sold domestically must come from domestic sources, including both parts and labor; otherwise a nearly prohibitive tariff or domestic consumption tax must be paid.

The basic economics of mixing regulations and domestic content requirements is essentially the same. Such schemes achieve protection of domestic producers without as much consumption restriction as tariffs or quotas that elevate internal prices across the board. This is because lower-priced imports are blended, at least to some extent, with costlier, protected domestic output. Hence the average price of the final good may be higher than free trade levels but lower than if equivalent producer protection were provided by a tariff, quota, or variable levy.

With tariffs, quotas, variable levies, and even deficiency payments, there are two prices to consider—the lower world price and the higher domestic producer price. With tariffs, quotas, and variable levies, domestic buyers also face a higher internal producer price. With deficiency payments, consumers are able to buy at the lower world price, but a direct government subsidy of producers is required. Mixing regulations, quantity-link schemes, or domestic content programs all involve *three* prices or price-like values—the world price at which allowable imports are purchased; the higher, protected producer price; and the price paid by domestic consumers for the "blended" product. This price in a competitive economy is a weighted average of the other two prices. In the analysis that follows we examine the partial equilibrium economics of a simple mixing regulation.

Analytical Framework

Let us consider the analytics of a straightforward mixing regulation. To give this discussion a less abstract air, imagine that we are considering a mixing regulation involving imported and domestic oranges to be made into frozen concentrate for juice. Imagine that the importing nation, Nation B, is small in world citrus markets; it faces a perfectly flat excess supply function for oranges at p_w in Fig. 7.1. The domestic demand and supply functions for concentrated orange juice (expressed in terms of oranges) are D and S respectively. Let us suppose that the government of Nation B imposes a mixing regula-

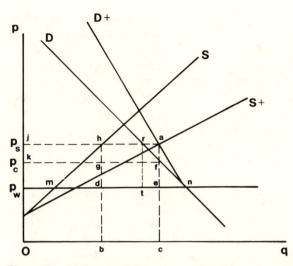

Figure 7.1 Mixing regulation or proportional import quota

tion on this market. The regulation limits the ratio of imports to domestic oranges in frozen concentrate to no more than r. This ratio is greater than zero. If the regulation calls for imports to be, say, no more than half as large as the domestic volume of all oranges used in frozen concentrate, $r = 0.5$; if it were to be a fourth as large, $r = 0.25$; if imports were to be no more than twice as large as the domestic portion, $r = 2.0$.

Each value of r can be translated easily into a domestic content value for the product. The domestic content value v is the minimum share that homegrown oranges must comprise in all concentrate sold. This relationship is

$$v = \frac{1}{1 + r}$$

and v is between 0 and $+ 1$. The following tabulation illustrates the relation between various r's and the corresponding values of v.

Ratio of imports to domestic quantity (r)	Domestic content of final product (v)
0.00	1.00 (100%)
0.25	0.80 (80%)
0.50	0.67 (67%)
0.75	0.57 (57%)
1.00	0.50 (50%)
2.00	0.33 (33%)
4.00	0.20 (20%)

Although either r or v can be used as the basis for analysis and discussion of proportional quotas, we will consider r as the mixing regulation decision to be made by the government.

The imposition of r as an import control measure can be managed in numerous ways. For now, imagine that import licenses are issued as specific certificates to domestic orange producers in relation to their output and sales or to processors in relation to their purchases of domestic materials. These licenses can be used directly by the producers or processors or sold freely to importing merchants. For our example, assume that producers of frozen orange juice are issued import licenses in some fixed proportion (r) to their purchases of domestic oranges.

Now consider the function labeled $S+$ in Fig. 7.1. It is the domestic supply curve S plus the horizontal addition, at each price, of the domestic quantity supplied at that price times r. Therefore, $S+$ is equal to $(1 + r)S$. The function $S+$ is a schedule of total supplies that can be available internally at various domestic *producer prices*. It includes domestic output plus allowable imports under the mixing regulation (r).

Now consider how the domestic *consumption price* is formed. The marginal cost of each unit available to buyers is a weighted average of the domestic producer price and the world import price. (Ignore the per-unit cost of processing.) The weights are formed from the mixing regulation r. That is, each unit of orange juice available to consumers will contain the minimum equivalent of $1 / 1 + r$ units of domestic oranges and $r / 1 + r$ units of imported oranges. We assume for this discussion that competition in the domestic market will keep the consumption price equal to the constrained marginal cost of the blended product. Hence, the following equation must hold:

$$p_c = \frac{1}{1 + r} p_s + \frac{r}{1 + r} p_w \tag{7.1}$$

or, in terms of the domestic content equivalent v,

$$p_c = v p_s + (1 - v) p_w \tag{7.2}$$

where p_c is any consumption price measured along D, p_s is the corresponding domestic producer price, and p_w is the world price. Rearrangement of Eq. (7.1) gives

$$p_s = p_c + r(p_c - p_w) \tag{7.3}$$

This price relation allows us to form $D+$ in Fig. 7.1. At each amount consumed internally and measured along the horizontal axis, $D+$ lies above D by the per-unit value $r(p_c - p_w)$. This function, $D+$, is a schedule of various *producer prices* (p_s) that are consistent with (1) each consumption price (p_c)

along D, (2) the fixed world price, and (3) the mixing regulation (r).

The intersection of $S+$ and $D+$ forms the equilibrium *producer price* and the equilibrium total quantity of domestic output plus allowable imports that can be sold along D when the world price is p_w. In Fig. 7.1, this intersection is at point a. The specific domestic producer price in this illustration is p_s and production is $0b$. Imports are bc, and $bc/0b = r$. The total supply $0c$ is sold domestically at the consumption price p_c. Figure 7.1 shows the three distinct prices (or per-unit values)—the low world price p_w, the high producer protected price p_s, and the middle-range consumer price p_c.

Because scarce import quotas are issued, economic rent is earned by the domestic interests who receive them. The rent arises as a consequence of producing $0b$ units domestically. On a per-unit basis the quota rent is $p_c - p_w$. In total, the rental value is *gfed*. Because the volume of imports is proportional to domestic production and because the quota rent $p_c - p_w$ is proportional to $p_s - p_c$, the quota rent in total (*gfed*) is exactly the total amount by which domestic output is subsidized (*jhgk*). The quota rent is the production subsidy. In fact, proportional quotas generate the same protective effects and economic consequences that would occur if a tariff equal to $p_c - p_w$ or *fe* in Fig. 7.1 were applied to all imports and then all tariff revenues paid over to domestic producers in relation to their production.

If the mixing regulation is changed, the results change as $S+$ and $D+$ change position. For instance, if r is reduced, the role of imports is diminished and the role of domestic production is enhanced. In this case, $S+$ and $D+$ rotate toward S and D respectively. The economic results more closely resemble autarky. As domestic production expands, imports fall, p_c approaches p_s, and both approach the intersection of D and S. If r is zero, autarky or full self-sufficiency prevails.

If r is increased, the allowable imports per unit of domestic production or sales expand; the scheme becomes less protective. As r increases, both $S+$ and $D+$ rotate clockwise, imports expand, and production falls as p_s approaches p_c and both approach p_w. At some increased value of r, the mixing regulation is no longer binding and the free trade equilibrium prevails at p_w with imports equal to *mn*.

Welfare Aspects

Proportional quotas generate rather interesting welfare gains and losses. As with all trade policy interventions, social losses occur in our partial equilibrium context. However, proportional quotas produce smaller overall losses than tariffs or quotas for a given amount of producer price protection, but larger losses than deficiency payments.

Refer again to Fig. 7.1. Technical efficiency losses equal to the triangle *hdm* occur on the supply side as production resources are pulled into the protected sector and other output is sacrificed elsewhere in the economy. These efficiency losses at p_s are the same for tariffs, quotas, variable levies, deficiency payments, and proportional quotas when the internal price is p_w. The triangle *hdm* is comparable to area *B* in Fig. 5.5. Consequently, the welfare differences among these policies involve (1) the presence and size of the consumer deadweight losses associated with higher prices, and (2) the redistribution aspects of the various policies among groups in the economy.

The proportional quota of Fig. 7.1 produces consumer deadweight losses of *fne*. This value, based on the middle-range consumption price of p_c, is less than if p_s were sustained by a tariff, a traditional quota, or a variable levy. In these latter cases, the deadweight loss would be the larger area indicated by *rnt* in Fig. 7.1.

Proportional quotas provide a production subsidy to domestic producers that arises out of the rent on scarce import quotas. Consumers sustain losses because the binding import quotas mean that average prices for buyers are higher than if free trade prevails. No direct redistribution of economic value through the government treasury occurs. Hence taxpayers are not openly affected. The establishment and operation of a mechanism to issue the proportional import quotas and manage their redemption would be, of course, a government responsibility and cost.

DIRECT PRODUCTION SUBSIDIES

Deficiency payments and variable levies ensure producers a guaranteed price for their output. The price guarantee is maintained by treasury disbursements in the case of deficiency payments and by flexible import duties when variable levies are in force. Each of these schemes might be viewed as having an output price (hence income) goal for producers as their central purpose. Direct production subsidies, on the other hand, are most often employed when domestic output expansion is sought, perhaps in a program of deliberate import substitution.

When importing nations embark on a program to promote an "infant" industry or sector, production subsidies are an alternative to tariffs or quotas. Direct production subsidies occur in two main ways. The first is as a specific payment from the government treasury *per unit* of the protected item, paid directly to the producer. The second occurs as a subsidy on one or more critical inputs like fertilizer, livestock feed, irrigation water, or machinery services. The latter intervention can be managed either by lowering the input price below the free market value or by making direct payments to buyers of the targeted input based on their use of it.

The effect of a production subsidy of this kind, no matter how implemented, is to reduce direct production costs. With no other changes occurring, this cost reduction will tend to spur domestic output at the expense of imports. Treasury outlays will be increased to cover the subsidy payments. A larger share of the domestic market will be captured by local industry. Self-sufficiency will increase, but at an expanded cost to taxpayers.

As part of a complex agricultural or farm policy mix, many nations provide indirect subsidies to agriculture for a variety of social objectives. Among these are a general desire to (1) keep people on the land or in rural areas, (2) enhance the amenities of rural life, (3) overcome costs of distance and uncertain weather, (4) give special protection to natural resources such as soil and water, and (5) provide agricultural research benefits to people and farms that would not otherwise be available.

These social objectives are pervasive around the world. They cause special institutions to be created for providing (1) cheap power and water to farmers, (2) agricultural research and extension services, (3) low-cost education and training for rural residents, (4) low-cost transportation for farm goods, and (5) other indirect benefits. That these benefits are really indirect production subsidies is not at issue. They may not be particularly pointed at import substitution, but they will have that effect. Yet these effects are quite hard to measure, even in principle. Hence, such general subsidies lie outside our purview since they are usually nonspecific in a commodity sense. Moreover, they are difficult to assess and balance from one sector of an economy to another since agriculture is usually not the only recipient of indirect subsidies.

Analytical Framework

The partial equilibrium analysis of a production subsidy is straightforward, paralleling the arguments associated with deficiency payments. The difference is that the direct production subsidy is established as a definite per-unit amount rather than as an output price guarantee. Figure 7.2 illustrates this policy intervention for the small-nation case.

The production subsidy is established per unit of the output of q. It is shown as s in Fig. 7.2a. As mentioned, this subsidy could be paid directly to the producers of q or it could take the form of an artifically lowered price for an input used in the production of q. For example, the government might pay a direct production subsidy of, say, 20 cents per bushel of corn to farmers. Or it might intervene somehow to lower the average market price of mixed fertilizer to corn growers. In modern corn production, this might involve a fertilizer price reduction of about 7.5 cents per pound.

Either approach will cause the short-run supply curve (S) to shift vertically downward at each price-output combination by 20 cents per bushel. This is because farmers' marginal costs fall. This new, subsidy-influenced supply curve is indicated as S^* in Fig. 7.2a. It differs from S vertically by the amount of the subsidy (s). The function S^* is the schedule of market supply prices for various quantities of q *after* the production subsidy is paid to domestic producers.

The horizontal difference between D and S^* in Fig. 7.2a is the function ED^* in Fig. 7.2b. This new, lower excess-demand function is now the demand for imports facing foreign sellers after the effects of the production subsidy are accounted for. The horizontal difference between *ED* and *ED** is the same as the horizontal difference between *S* and *S**.

In this case, imports drop from *ac* to *ab* at the international price of p_1 (Fig. 7.2*b*). This fall in imports exactly matches the expansion in domestic output, which is *de* in Fig. 7.2*a*. The cost-lowering effects of the subsidy are responsible for this increase in domestic output. The production subsidy is *fe* per unit produced, and its total value is illustrated by the shaded zone in Fig. 7.2*a*.

Per-unit returns to domestic producers, including the subsidy, increase from p_1 to p_2. These higher returns induce an expansion in output and an inflow of variable resources into the subsidized sector. The resulting reduction in imports has no direct effect on buyers of the subsidized product since this fall in imports is exactly balanced by an increase in domestic production. Prices to buyers of the product do not change.

Welfare Gains and Losses

In this small-nation scenario, the economic welfare aspects are identical with those occurring under deficiency payments. Producers gain, taxpayers are burdened, and the broader society sacrifices output elsewhere as movable resources enter the sector. As long as international prices are not influenced by the change in the nation's imports, consumers remain, in principle, unaffected by the subsidy.

In the large-nation case, not illustrated here, the application of a production subsidy could drive the international price below p_1 in Fig. 7.2. Imagine, for instance, a positively sloped *ES(R)* function through point *c*. Consumers will demand more, but this will involve less additional volume than domestic producers will produce behind the subsidy. Hence, imports will fall as consumers benefit from lower prices of the subsidized product.

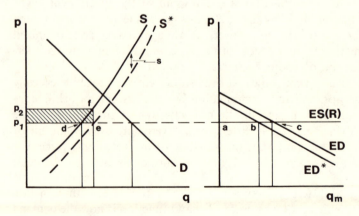

Figure 7.2   Direct production subsidy

SUMMARY

Proportional quotas, sometimes called mixing regulations or domestic content schemes, link permitted imports to domestic production and sales. This kind of protective trade policy causes consumer prices to exceed world levels but allows them to remain lower than if an equivalent amount of producer protection were provided by a tariff or a quota. Production subsidy via a mixing regulation occurs because consumer prices are higher than world prices and because producers are able to capture the scarcity value of the proportional import quotas.

Direct production subsidies lower the per-unit supply costs of the protected item. Output itself may be subsidized or the cost of one or more important inputs may be artificially lowered. The result is an expansion of output, a reduction of imports, and an outflow from the government treasury. Consumer prices may or may not be lowered. Production subsidies are sometimes referred to in these circumstances as implicit import tariffs.

QUESTIONS

7.1 Upper Revolta has a small, high-cost farm machinery industry. This sector is protected as an infant industry by means of domestic content regulations that require that at least 50 percent of the value added of all farm machines sold internally must come from domestic sources. The government plans to phase out this protection by reducing the domestic content regulation by 10 percent annually—from 50 percent to 40 percent to 30 percent, etc. Analyze and describe the economic implications of this policy.

7.2 Use some simple diagrams and reasoning to show how and why a deficiency payment scheme for producers, supported entirely by the proceeds of an import tariff, is exactly equivalent in its economic effects to a mixing regulation that achieves the same production-input mix.

7.3 The nation of Wisteria, a small net importer, is proposing to levy a fixed per-unit *consumption* tax on vegetable oils. The main purpose is to drive the internal price of margarine up near the heavily supported butter price. This tax will be paid by all users, and the proceeds will go to the government. Illustrate and discuss the trade, production, price, and consumption aspects of this policy change, assuming that free trade in vegetable oils is the current situation. Compare this kind of policy with a domestic production subsidy that results in the same shrinkage of import volume.

7.4 The nation of Zerona is located in the northern latitudes but still maintains a small deciduous tree fruit industry (apples, pears, plums, etc.). The fruit growers of Zerona receive a fixed production subsidy per unit of deciduous fruit marketed. Even with this subsidy, Zerona still imports deciduous fruit from the world market. Illustrate and discuss how this policy for protection departs from free trade. Who gains? Who loses? Why?

ADDITIONAL READINGS

Corden, W. M. 1971. *The Theory of Protection*, Clarendon Press, Oxford, England, pp. 12–14 and 45–50. (Partial equilibrium analyses of quantity-linking schemes and domestic content requirements.)

Greenaway, D. 1983. *Trade Policy and the New Protectionism*, St. Martin's Press, New York, New York, pp. 143–145. (Protection by means of production subsidy is examined in partial equilibrium style.)

Grennes, T. 1984. *International Economics*, Prentice-Hall, Englewood Cliffs, New Jersey, pp. 227–228. (A short partial equilibrium look at the tariff versus production subsidy issue.)

Grossman, G. M. 1981. The theory of domestic content protection and content preference, *Quarterly Journal of Economics*, 96:583–603. (A rather advanced discussion of this topic, but one of the few available in the literature.)

Krauss, M. B. 1978. *The New Protectionism,* New York University Press, New York, New York, App. B. [A discussion of the tariff versus a production subsidy as a redistributive (protective) mechanism.]

McCulloch, R., and Johnson, H. G. 1973. A note on proportionally distributed quotas, *American Economic Review*, 63(4):726–32. [A rigorous but clear geometric presentation of proportional quotas (mixing regulations)—close to the spirit of the discussion in this chapter.]

Chapter 8

"Voluntary" Import Quotas and Other Administrative Trade Distortions

Since the 1940s, ordinary tariffs have dwindled in importance as trade-restricting devices. International negotiations have successfully cut away at traditional tariffs. For instance, the average tariff rate on all 1931 United States imports was equal to nearly 60 percent ad valorem. By 1948, it was down to 15 percent, and by 1984, it was only about 5 percent. Other trading nations display similar trends. However, an ingenious variety of nontariff measures has emerged to protect favored domestic producers by providing insulation from foreign competition. This is especially true in numerous agricultural product markets. Several of these nontariff trade policies are described and analyzed in previous chapters—import quotas, deficiency payments, variable levies, mixing regulations, and direct production subsidies. These measures are generally speaking open and deliberate government interventions whose specific purpose is to alter the market for imports into an individual nation. As such, they are subject to formal economic analysis and evaluation.

In addition, there are numerous other trade-influencing measures pursued by national governments whose effects are subtle but potentially quite effective in restricting or distorting international trade flows. It is this category of administrative nontariff trade barriers that seems to be growing and proliferating across international markets, including those for many agricultural products. We consider two main categories of such measures in this chapter. First, we examine the basic economics of "voluntary" quotas applied by exporting nations in response to pressures applied by large importers who wish to restrict inbound shipments of particular products without using traditional protective policies. Second, we will discuss without formal analysis the complex array of other administrative nontariff trade barriers that function behind the scenes in trading nations.

VOLUNTARY QUOTAS

From time to time, importing nations wish to protect domestic producers from strong import competition but do not want to impose new or more stringent tariffs or formal quotas. The reasons may be political, administrative, or because the need for protection is seen as temporary. In such cases, the import nation may determine a global import volume, then negotiate voluntary quotas with each of its exporting suppliers. Such a program is feasible only when the imports to be restricted come from a relatively few export nations.

The typical voluntary quota sets a maximum sales quantity for each cooperating exporter nation over the relevant time period—perhaps one year. Enforcement of each quota is conducted by authorities in the exporting nation, not the importing nation. Naturally, the importer government monitors compliance, but day-to-day management is in the hands of each cooperating exporter. For instance, if Nation A wishes to protect its beef producers from low-priced imports, it might negotiate voluntary quotas with its four main beef suppliers, Nations B, C, D, and E. Each of these nations agrees to limit its exports of beef to Nation A to an agreed-upon volume, the total of which is less than would occur under free or unrestricted trade. The authorities of Nations B, C, D, and E are responsible for controlling the amounts shipped to A. Nation A monitors the beef trade but does not directly intervene.

Why would these exporters agree to such voluntary limitations? First, they may fear that failure to cooperate would lead to more stringent, formal import quotas or other interventions enacted on a permanent basis. Second, there may be political or other noneconomic considerations between the nations, introducing a measure of coercion into trade policy discussions. That is, retaliation of one sort or another is anticipated by exporters if voluntary quotas are rejected. Third, there may be direct economic advantages to be gained by the cooperating exporters. These may offset the onerous aspects of import restrictions.

To illustrate this third aspect of voluntary quotas, consider a large importing nation, Nation A, dealing with a few exporters for the bulk of its purchases (Fig. 8.1). The small-nation situation is not generally suitable for the application of voluntary import quotas. In this illustration, imagine that all exporters agree "voluntarily" to limit their shipments to Nation A. The aggregate amount of the individual, voluntary national quotas is $\bar{q}$. This is a binding restriction since it is less than the free market volume of trade indicated by the intersection of *ED* and *ES(R)*. As a consequence, the price inside Nation A rises to p_2 and the supply price to export sellers drops to p_1. The inherent scarcity of the voluntary quotas produces rent value equal to the shaded area in Fig. 8.1. This is similar to the analytical results of traditional quotas.

However, the interesting feature about this voluntary quota rent is that it flows to exporters who hold the scarce quotas. In principle, these quota rents are acquired by firms or government agencies in the exporting nations who manage the restriction or who are granted the scarce shipping privileges. They purchase or produce the restricted product at p_1 and sell it inside Nation A at p_2. The international transfer of these windfall gains from the importer, Nation A, to the cooperating exporters helps to explain why exporting nations often agree to voluntary quotas.

In economic welfare terms, the operation of a voluntary quota scheme produces even larger net social losses for the importer than if the same restrictions were achieved by a traditional quota or tariff. Recall Fig. 5.5. In addition to the net social losses reflected in areas B and D of that figure, area C (or, more accurately, *all* tariff revenue or quota rent) also is lost to individuals in the importer nation. It is acquired by the quota holders in the export nation. With voluntary quotas, area C represents a loss of consumer surplus in the importing nation that is not gained by anyone else in that nation via redistribution. Common sense suggests that area C may be quite large relative to areas B and D if imports represent a significant part of total consumption and/or the excess demand is inelastic.

ADMINISTRATIVE TRADE DISTORTIONS

Tariffs, quotas, mixing regulations, and other overt trade policy schemes (including voluntary quotas) involve open and public expressions of intent by national governments to restrict or distort international trade. Such overtures may bring criticism and even retaliation from affected trading partners. Hence, an intricate and often subtle network of administrative trade barriers may evolve

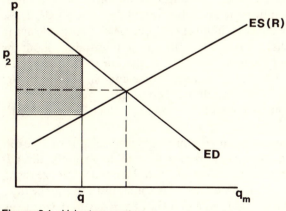

Figure 8.1 Voluntary quotas

within importing nations to discourage or additionally burden foreign goods as they move onto domestic markets.

Since administrative trade distortions can originate from deep within government bureaucracies, they are not easy to analyze in terms of supply, demand, and price effects. Moreover, the bulk of administrative restraints and distortions grows out of discriminatory and overzealous application of basically sensible regulations designed to protect the consuming public from unhealthy, dangerous, or improperly represented products. Although they can be very important to the trading community, these distortions operate on the periphery of formal trade policy. They may not even reflect deliberate decisions by the ruling political leadership. Hence their role is complex, difficult to measure, and troublesome to negotiate on a broad front.

There are numerous ways to classify and describe these nontariff, administrative barriers to agricultural trade. None is fully satisfactory, but the following, simple listing may be helpful in visualizing the character of these barriers.

    1 Health and sanitary regulations
    2 Import licensing procedures
    3 Advance security deposits on orders for import goods
    4 Prepayment of internal excise taxes
    5 Container size and packaging material requirements
    6 Labeling and marketing regulations
    7 Material or industrial standards
    8 Discrimination against imports in government procurement procedures
    9 Changes in customs valuation of imported goods
    10 Complex customs formalities and reporting requirements
    11 Requirements for submission and evaluation of product samples

When any of these or other administrative measures are applied in a way that consistently and systematically discriminates against imported goods, they can be viewed as trade barriers. When that happens, imported products bear additional costs not sustained by more favorably treated domestic goods. These extra costs appear as either direct or indirect cash charges, as costly delays in the movement of merchandise through the system, or as uncertainty about the availability and final price of imported goods in relation to their domestic counterparts. All of these factors tend to inhibit trade and narrow the market for imports in relation to locally produced goods. In extreme cases, administrative barriers can completely exclude foreign products from domestic markets.

The existence and precise effect of administrative trade distortions are difficult to document and measure. Exporters will tend to magnify the administrative impediments they face, and importers will tend to minimize them, especially their alleged discriminatory effects. Also, administrative procedures or the interpretation of existing regulations can shift from day to day or week to week as political attitudes or market conditions change. Administrative trade barriers can rise or fall, tighten or relax, without any overt, formal action being taken by government leaders.

SUMMARY

In addition to formal, deliberate market interventions, there are numerous other ways that national governments can restrict or distort international trade. These measures range from voluntary quotas (or import limitations) arranged with major foreign suppliers to administrative trade barriers applied from within the government bureaucracies responsible for trade transactions. Administrative actions applied in a discriminatory way discourage imports by increasing importers' direct or indirect marketing costs, by creating lengthy delays in handling imported goods, or by injecting additional uncertainties into the commercial process for foreign sellers. Administrative trade barriers can rise or fall without formal actions being taken by the importing nation's government.

QUESTIONS

8.1 The government of Microbia says it wants to be sure that both imported and domestic dairy products do not contain disease-causing bacteria. Rigid sanitary regulations and testing requirements are established for foreign dairy products before they can be released for domestic distribution. Exporters argue that Microbian products are subject to less stringent requirements, making per-unit production and marketing costs for imports higher than for similar domestic products. Assume that the exporters are correct. Illustrate the economic implications and effects of this situation using partial equilibrium demand and supply functions.

8.2 Industria is the world's largest importer of coal even though it has a sizable coal mining sector of its own. For years, Industria has levied a fixed tariff on coal imports. Recently, this tariff has not provided sufficient producer protection, in the eyes of the government. Not wishing to institute new tariffs or formal import controls, the Industrian government negotiated voluntary import limitations with the two countries that together supply 98 percent of its imports—Carbona and Mineland. These voluntary quotas, combined with the existing tariff, elevate coal prices inside Industria to values acceptable to the government. Illustrate and discuss the trade, price, and welfare effects on Carbona and Mineland.

8.3 Imagine that two grades of coal are supplied by Carbona and Mineland—high and low. Industria's demand for high-grade coal is much more price inelastic than that for low-grade coal. However, the voluntary quotas do not recognize these quality differences. They are global quotas—"coal is coal." Discuss how the composition of coal imports into Industria would be affected by these voluntary quotas.

8.4 Administrative trade distortions usually are visualized as nontariff *import* barriers. However, exports also could be affected by similar administrative actions. List and discuss some plausible ways that exports of a primary agricultural commodity could be affected by such informal measures. Consider actions that might favor domestic producers on the one hand or domestic consumers on the other.

ADDITIONAL READINGS

Anjaria, S. J., Iqbal, Z., Kirmani, N., and Perez, L. L. 1983. Developments in International Trade Policy, International Monetary Fund Occasional Paper No. 6, International Monetary Fund, Washington, D.C. (July 1983). (Part IV and App. I focus on agricultural trade policies affecting major commodities.)

Caves, R. E., and Jones, R. W. 1981. *World Trade and Payments: An Introduction*, 3rd ed. Little, Brown and Co., Boston, Massachusetts, pp. 246–248. (Basically the same argument as in this chapter.)

Food and Agriculture Organization of the United Nations. 1983. New Protectionism and Attempts at Liberalization in Agricultural Trade, FAO Economic and Social Development Paper No. 27, FAO, Rome. (Discussion of nontariff protectionism in agriculture with case studies; see the classification scheme on p. 2.)

Greenaway, D. 1983. *Trade Policy and the New Protectionism*, St. Martin's Press, New York, New York, Chaps. 7–9. (An economic view of the emergence, extent, and consequences of nontariff interventions, including a discussion of voluntary quotas on pp. 138–140.)

Grennes, T. 1984. *International Economics*, Prentice-Hall, Englewood Cliffs, New Jersey, pp. 187–190. (This section discusses voluntary quotas.)

Hillman, J. S. 1978. *Non-Tariff Agricultural Trade Barriers*, University of Nebraska Press, Lincoln, Nebraska. (A major source book on nontariff barriers in agricultural trade; see especially the taxonomy in Chap. 4.)

Middleton, R. 1975. *Negotiating on Non-Tariff Distortions of Trade*, St. Martin's Press, New York, New York, Chaps. 2 and 15. (Descriptions of "quantitative, para-tariff, fiscal, administrative, technical, and other distortions of trade" mainly within the European Free Trade Area.)

Chapter 9

Import and Consumption Subsidies

Most of the agricultural trade policy schemes in force around the world are directed in one way or another toward producer protection. Their costs are borne by consumers, taxpayers, the rest of society, and foreign sellers. However, some trade interventions on the import side strive to benefit the consumers or users of foreign products. These are import or consumption subsidies. When used, they tend to lower domestic prices and therefore promote consumption of the favored product. These objectives are achieved at the expense of tax-payers, domestic producers, or both.

Though the distinction is not clear-cut, we can identify two main categories of agricultural products that are likely candidates for import or consumption subsidies. The first category might include crucially important staple food prod-ucts that are consumed by low-income, vulnerable groups—perhaps rice con-sumed by poor urban wage earners or wheat for unemployed or underemployed peasants. These particular examples suggest that import or consumption sub-sidies for staple products are mostly to be encountered in low-income, food-deficit, developing nations. In fact, such schemes may be funded partly or whol-ly by foreign donor nations engaged in programs of technical and economic assistance.

The second category includes agricultural production inputs like fertilizer, chemicals, hybrid seeds, and machinery. The idea behind such subsidies is to reduce the direct production costs of commodities for which they are inputs. In reducing the direct supply price of these commodities, self-sufficiency in or even exports of the favored final products are promoted. As we discussed in Chap. 7, deliberately reduced input costs via an import or consumption subsidy also can be viewed as a production subsidy from the standpoint of protected growers.

However, if we wish to focus on the markets for the import- or consumption-subsidized inputs themselves, we can visualize the relevant input demand functions as "derived demands." Derived demands for productive inputs in agriculture have their origin in the technical production processes and prices for the final commodities in which they are employed. For example, the demand for agricultural fertilizers depends on the per-unit value of the extra output of corn, wheat, or cotton that successive additional applications of those fertilizers generate.

The partial equilibrium economics of import-promoting interventions is basically the same no matter what kind of products are being subsidized. First we will consider import subsidies, then consumption (or user) subsidies. Then we will examine the partial equilibrium welfare aspects of these policy schemes.

IMPORT SUBSIDY

Assume that the government of Nation K decides to subsidize the importation of rice to benefit low-income urban workers and their families. We can easily suppose that this group within the society of Nation K is a large and perhaps politically unstable element. The partial equilibrium analysis of such an import subsidy scheme is shown in Fig. 9.1.

Instead of a tariff on imports, the subsidy program provides a payment to import merchants or firms of the per-unit amount s. This payment is made on each ton of rice imported. The impact of this subsidy is to shift Nation K's excess demand curve from ED to ED^* (Fig. 9.1b). The vertical distance between ED^* and ED is the subsidy amount s. The effective rice import demand function shifts to the right because the subsidy enables importers to buy rice at the world price and sell at a lower price inside Nation K. The subsidy initially will allow imports to undercut domestic rice prices.

As internal prices fall, the quantity demanded domestically expands, but domestic production decreases. Subsidy-induced rice imports expand to fill the gap. The total cost of the government's import subsidy is the per unit subsidy s times the new, higher volume of imports.

In Fig. 9.1, imports increase from the equivalent of ab to cd (Fig. 9.1b). The small-nation assumption, as reflected in this illustration, means that international rice prices remain at p_1, but internal prices fall to p_2, and $p_2 = p_1 - s$. Total subsidy outlays are indicated by the shaded area $aedc$ in Fig. 9.1b. On the domestic market in Nation K, the subsidy-induced price decrease causes domestic rice production to fall along S from point f to point g. Domestic rice consumption expands along D from point h to point j. Original imports are fh in Fig. 9.1a, but with the subsidy, imports expand to gj. Observe that

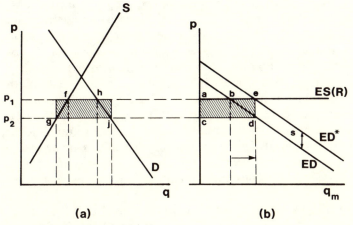

Figure 9.1 Import subsidy

$fh = ab$ and $gh = cd$. Total import subsidy outlays are also shown as a shaded area in Fig. 9.1a.

A monopolistic, government rice-importing board could easily provide an import subsidy equivalent to s by making domestic rice sales at p_2, having purchased its import inventory at p_1. The subsidy value $aecd$ would appear in the board's financial accounts as a net loss on rice import transactions. The smaller the role imports play in total domestic consumption, the smaller the subsidy required to keep internal prices down. However, if imports are relatively small, domestic rice producers bear a large share of the burden for keeping internal prices low.

It is also worth noting that when an import subsidy is in operation, some method to control *exports* must be in place. This is because the domestic, subsidized market price is lower than the international price. In the absence of such export controls, producers or merchants would be anxious to buy supplies at low internal prices and sell them internationally at higher world prices.

DIRECT CONSUMPTION SUBSIDY

As a price-decreasing policy, a consumption subsidy bears a similar relationship to the import subsidy as a production subsidy bears to the tariff in raising producer prices. A consumption subsidy is a direct payment (or some form of rebate) that lowers the per-unit consumption cost of the affected commodity to all users. Imports are not directly affected, but they are indirectly stimulated. A consumption subsidy can be and is applied to staple food products like rice or wheat with much the same motivation as the import subsidy example just discussed. However, in the following illustration we consider a consumption subsidy for a production input.

Assume that Nation L embarks on a policy designed to expand its production of bananas for export. As part of this effort, the government chooses to subsidize the application of pest control chemicals used in modern banana cultivation. All users of these products, which we assume are partly imported and partly produced domestically, are given a cash rebate (or bounty) from the government on presentation of appropriate purchase receipts.

Figure 9.2 illustrates the partial equilibrium aspects of this policy on the assumption that Nation L is a large purchaser of these particular chemicals on the international market. Because the consumption subsidy s applies to all users, the effective domestic market demand moves rightward from D to D^*, a vertical distance s (Fig. 9.2a). This is because more chemicals are demanded at each market price or, stated another way, the market demand price for chemicals is increased at each consumption amount because of the available subsidy.

An effect of this increase in domestic market demand is to shift the excess demand function to the right, from ED to ED^* (Fig. 9.2b). The horizontal distance of this latter shift at each price is the same as the horizontal movement of D to D^*. This import demand expansion boosts the international price from p_1 to p_2 as imports expand by the amount ab. The availability of the subsidy pushes the internal user's per-unit cost of chemicals down to p_3, where $p_3 = p_2 - s$. However, the international market price still rules for market transactions inside Nation L. So, although there is a net increase in domestic consumption of amount ab, there is no negative production effect. Actually, the supply price to domestic chemical producers increases from p_1 to p_2 as a consequence of the large-nation assumption and the subsidy-induced expansion in domestic demand.

Two "prices" prevail inside Nation L for agricultural chemicals. One is

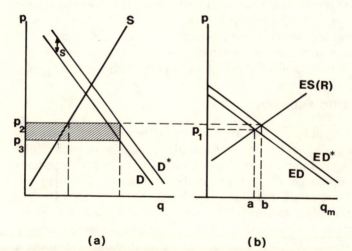

(a)   (b)

Figure 9.2 Consumption subsidy

p_2, the market price of chemicals at which actual purchases and sales are made. The second is p_3, the lower net price to buyers, including the subsidy. The total consumption subsidy is shown in Fig. 9.2a as the shaded area. The consumption subsidy basically transfers value away from taxpayers toward users of the favored commodity.

As the ratio between imports and domestic consumption increases, the import subsidy approaches the consumption subsidy in its overall effects. In the extreme case, where there is no domestic production of the subsidized product, import and consumption subsidies become exactly the same. This is because the excess demand (*ED*) on which an import subsidy is paid becomes the same as the domestic demand (*D*) on which a consumption subsidy is paid.

WELFARE EFFECTS

We explore the partial equilibrium welfare aspects of import and consumption subsidies with the same basic approach we used for import tariffs and quotas. In Fig. 9.3, *D* and *S* are domestic demand and supply functions respectively. The unsubsidized price is p_1, and p_2 is the per-unit value in the domestic market after the subsidy is applied.

First consider the import subsidy. In this case, the price to both consumers and producers falls from p_1 to p_2. Buyers gain the area $A + B + C + D + E$ in added consumers' surplus. Producers lose the area $A + E$ in producer surplus value. Taxpayers cover subsidy payment costs, which amount to $E + B + C + D + F$. Netting out gains and losses, we see that the society sustains net losses equivalent in value to the areas E and F.

The area E reflects a net loss of producer surplus occurring as the fixed factors of production in the domestic economy are underutilized because of the artificially low price. The area F is difficult to describe simply. It is that part of the government payment used to acquire the product at p_1 and sell it domestically at p_2, which is not reflected in additional consumer surplus. This occurs because the larger amount of q demanded at p_2 would not be purchased at p_1.

The welfare effects of a consumption subsidy are slightly different. Recall that in this case, consumers benefit from the lower price of p_2, which includes the subsidy. However, the market price to domestic producers remains at p_1. Consumer surplus increases by the area $A + B + C + D + E$ in Fig. 9.3. Producers as a group neither gain nor lose, but taxpayers lose subsidy payments of $A + B + C + D + E + F$. This is because the subsidy covers all units consumed, not just those imported. The net social loss in this instance is only area F. Domestic producers do not lose producer surplus with the consumption subsidy as they do with the import subsidy.

These comparative results are qualitatively similar to welfare conclusions that emerge from comparing a tariff (or quota) to production subsidy payments.

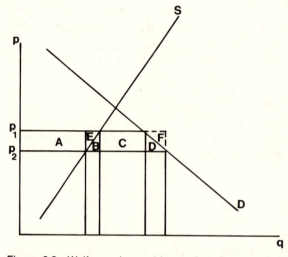

Figure 9.3 Welfare gains and losses from import subsidy

Both production and consumption subsidies typically involve larger taxpayer outlays than occur with equally protective tariffs or import subsidies. But they entail smaller net social losses, there being no consumer surplus loss with a direct production subsidy and no producer surplus loss with a direct consumption subsidy.

SUMMARY

Nations may sometimes intervene to expand the import volume of selected products to keep domestic prices lower than they otherwise would be. Either an import or a consumption subsidy can accomplish this. Crucial, staple food products or imported agricultural inputs are likely candidates for such favored treatment. With either an import or consumption subsidy, domestic consumption expands, internal prices to buyers fall, and imports expand. Government expenditures will rise and, with an import subsidy, domestic production (if any) will fall.

The transfer of economic value that occurs with this kind of trade policy involves gains by consumers of the favored products at the expense of the taxpayers, domestic producers, or both. As with other trade policy schemes, there are net social losses. They can be viewed as the society's costs of pursuing the price-reducing, consumption-expanding goals of import or consumption subsidies.

QUESTIONS

9.1 Niceland decides to apply a fixed per-unit import subsidy to its purchases of feed grains from the world market. This subsidy is available to all Nicelandic importers, who are numerous. Discuss and illustrate the economics of this policy assuming that Niceland is a large importer of feed grains from the world market and also has numerous domestic feed grain producers. Who benefits and who is injured by this policy? Why might such a policy be adopted by the Nicelandic government?

9.2 How would your analysis of the previous question change if the Nicelandic government adopted a generally equivalent ad valorem import subsidy based on world corn prices?

9.3 Government officials of the developing nation of Aquador have decided to keep the price of its staple food commodity, wheat, low and stable to benefit low-income wage earners. This decision was taken even though only about half of domestic wheat consumption comes from imports. The debate within Aquador is now focused on whether to pursue this policy by means of an import subsidy or a direct consumption subsidy available to all consumers of wheat. Advise the government as a trade policy economist.

9.4 The nation of Fiberia wishes to promote and expand its cotton-growing sector. To do this, it has decided to subsidize its imports of cotton harvesting machines. The Fiberian parliament has appropriated a fixed annual fund to be used for this purpose. Illustrate the economics of this policy and its accompanying constraint, knowing that Fiberia is a relatively small importer of farm machinery on the world market and has no domestic farm machinery industry.

ADDITIONAL READINGS

Grennes, T. 1984. *International Economics*, Prentice-Hall, Englewood Cliffs, New Jersey, pp. 218–222. (Discussion of an import subsidy in partial equilibrium style.)

Part Three

Protection by Exporters

The greatest meliorator of the world is selfish, huckstering trade.

Ralph Waldo Emerson

Chapter 10

Export Expansion with Price Guarantees, Subsidies, and Promotion

It would be a serious mistake to think that only importing nations can protect either their producers or consumers by intervention in agricultural trade. Export trade policy offers a rich tradition of elaborate and effective schemes for protection. So in the next few chapters we turn our attention from importers' trade policy to exporters' trade policy. First we will examine several schemes designed to protect domestic producers. Then we will look at some designed to protect domestic buyers of an exported good. Naturally, any export protection or export control scheme will have economic effects that extend beyond its immediate goals. We will consider these effects.

EXPORT EXPANSION AND DUMPING

Export expansion is a powerful theme in the agricultural and trade policies of many nations. Though exports may be taxed or occasionally controlled, more often than not the underlying goal of public policy over the long run is to seek overseas outlets for expanding farm production. Large and growing exports for surplus agricultural producing nations are associated with strong farm prices and the accumulation of foreign exchange earnings.

The subject of this chapter and the next is how export producer protection via trade policy operates. The basic line of discussion in this chapter is how special support or protection for producers in agricultural exporting nations leads to output expansion. This output growth is pushed wholly or partly onto world markets by means of one trade policy scheme or another. Here we will consider the economics of export subsidies, the export consequences of production subsidies, the role of export promotion as a deliberate policy and, finally, food aid and trade expansion.

When countries pursue an expansionary trade policy, they are sometimes accused of export "dumping" by importer countries whose domestic products are displaced by lower-priced imports. Dumping allegations also may be leveled by competing exporters whose traditional markets are captured by the expansionary exporter. There is no precise or widely accepted economic definition of dumping. However, there are two general ways by which export dumping is identified and described. One occurs when the good being exported is sold abroad to some buyers at prices lower than those charged either to domestic buyers or to other importers. A second occurs when the export good is sold abroad at a price less than its cost of production. Although the second criterion is often difficult to establish with clarity, the first is relatively straightforward.

A pervasive consequence of export dumping is that the dumping nation's exports are larger than they would be without it. As we shall see, trading nations that pursue export and production subsidies usually can be said to be dumping.

EXPORT SUBSIDIES

Export subsidies, even when not masquerading under other names, come in numerous forms. They may be specific, as fixed or ad valorem payments made on the volumes exported. In this case, they are the reverse, in trade policy economics, of fixed or ad valorem import tariffs. They may be open-ended or variable payments. Then they are the reverse of the variable import levy.

Export subsidies occur when the government gives an exporter a direct per-unit payment on the volume of goods cleared for foreign destinations. Such a payment enables an export firm to purchase the product internally at a higher price and sell it externally at a lower price.

Export subsidies also can be provided indirectly by marketing agencies or boards that buy on the domestic market and have monopoly rights to sell on the international market. Such agencies provide an export subsidy if they purchase a commodity at a higher price domestically than they sell it internationally.

If the export subsidy is specific in its per-unit amount, the internal market price rides above the international price by the subsidy amount. If the internal market price is fixed (guaranteed), the per-unit subsidy must fluctuate to accommodate the difference between internal and world prices. In the first instance, the export subsidy is like a tariff. In the second, it resembles a variable import levy.

Specific Export Subsidy

Consider first an export subsidy whose per-unit value is a specified amount. Such an export subsidy might take the form of a cash payment to the exporter upon shipment of the product in question, or it might be a rebate or exemption from a domestic sales or excise tax. It might also occur as subsidized access to credit, which lowers exporting costs by a specific per-unit amount. For example, a fixed export subsidy on butter from Nation A might be the equivalent of, say, 50 cents per kilogram no matter what the size of the shipment or its international destination. This intervention would ensure that the domestic price was 50 cents per kilogram higher than the world price expressed net of transfer and transportation costs.

The economics of a fixed export subsidy is depicted in Fig. 10.1 for a small export nation. Since our attention is now on the export side, we draw the excess supply curve of the nation in question as ES in the right-hand quadrant of Fig. 10.1. The horizontal excess demand curve for the rest of the trading world is $ED(R)$.

The per-unit export subsidy is shown as the vertical distance s in Fig. 10.1b. Its effect is to lower the supply price of exports by the value of s per unit, generating a new excess supply curve faced by foreign buyers, ES^*. The new intersection of ES^* with $ED(R)$ indicates an expansion of export volume by an amount equal to ab. The small-nation assumption employed here means that the international price remains at p_1, but internal prices increase. This increase in domestic prices occurs as exporters, eager to earn subsidy payments, expand export sales and bid up prices paid for export goods. In this simple illustration, $p_2 = p_1 + s$. (There is no reason why the value of s could not be set in some ad valorem relation with p_1.)

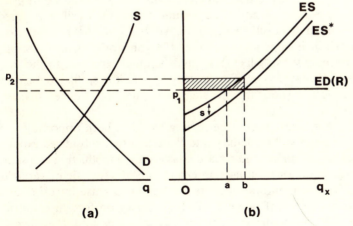

Figure 10.1   Fixed export subsidy

As domestic market prices increase, internal consumption is curtailed but production expands (Fig. 10.1*a)*. Hence, exports can and do increase. Export subsidy outlays are shown as the shaded area in Fig. 10.1*b*. They can occur as outright government expenditures or as excise tax revenues foregone.

When an exporting nation elevates a domestic market price above international levels, by whatever means and for whatever purpose, it must also curtail its imports of that product and its close substitutes. Otherwise, identical or similar products will flow into that nation seeking the higher domestic price. The government will find itself trying to support the international price for the whole world. This could be very expensive.

Variable Export Subsidy

Next consider the variable or open-ended export subsidy. The large-nation case is employed here for illustration and comparison (Fig. 10.2). The variable export subsidy is quite interesting from an agricultural policy viewpoint because its use fully disconnects domestic prices from world prices.

In Fig. 10.2*a,* the guaranteed domestic price for our illustrative commodity q is set at p_s. Note that p_s is assumed to be considerably higher than p_1, which is the free-market equilibrium price. At p_s, domestic production is stimulated and domestic consumption is curtailed compared with the situation at p_1. The excess supply function reflecting the guaranteed internal price p_s is vertical at ES^* for international prices below p_s. To move this additional excess supply volume onto the world market, suppose that an export subsidy is introduced. The quantity 0*e* (or *ab*) in Fig. 10.2*b* is the volume of exports required if p_s is to be the ruling and guaranteed domestic price.

This export volume 0*e* can only be exported at the lower international price p_2, where *ED(R)* and ES^* intersect. Because this particular export nation is large, exports above the free market amount will press the world price down below p_1. An export subsidy of *bc* per unit sold abroad will be required to maintain p_s. The total subsidy expenditure will be *abcd*. If the amount exported to maintain p_s is large and/or if the effect on world prices is sizable, an open-ended export subsidy like this could be quite expensive to the subsidizing government. Moreover, the subsidy expenditures, like deficiency payments, are a clear, obvious transfer item in the national budget, open to scrutiny by all.

Competing producers around the trading world in both importing and other exporting nations will be damaged to the extent that subsidized exports drive down international prices and replace nonsubsidized production and sales. Whenever a large trading nation uses an export subsidy, specific or variable, foreign nations with agricultural interests are bound to sense intrusion and damage. The public effect of one nation's trade policy on foreign countries is perhaps most obvious with export subsidies. This is because they involve overt, positive actions that depress international prices and narrow the market outlets for other producers.

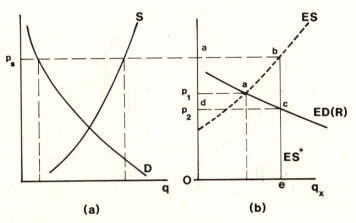

Figure 10.2 Variable export subsidy

The price- and market-depressing consequences of import restrictions are slightly more subtle since they arise because the restricting nations do not purchase as much as they otherwise would. This is less blatant than actually making unprofitable exports that directly result in lower world prices and drawing financial support for such expenditures from the public treasury.

Trade Reversal and Export Subsidy

A high enough price guarantee coupled with either an open-ended export subsidy or a large enough fixed subsidy can convert an importing nation into an exporter of the commodity in question. This can happen even without domestic supply or demand changes or changes in the international economy. This possibility is illustrated in Fig. 10.3, which depicts only the relevant international market. The horizontal axis registers imports to the left of 0 and exports to the right of 0. The particular nation's excess demand and supply function is shown as *ED-ES,* with point *f* as the isolation equilibrium price, at which neither exports nor imports occur.

For convenience only, imagine that this nation is small in the world market so that the world price p_1 corresponds to the excess supply and demand function for the rest of the world, *ES(R)-ED(R)*. With no particular intervention by the government, this nation would import $0e$ units of q at the world price p_1. In this circumstance, p_1 also would be the domestic price.

Now suppose the government instituted a high, domestic price guarantee (p_s) for q and sustained it by an open-ended export subsidy plus appropriate import controls. Note that this guaranteed price is higher than the isolation equilibrium price *f.* At domestic prices below *f,* this nation is an importer, producing less than is demanded domestically. But domestic prices above *f* generate an excess supply. More is produced than is demanded internally. In the absence of other policy measures, this excess supply must be exported. At p_s in Fig. 10.3, the excess supply amount is indicated by $0f$ (or *ab*). The export subsidy

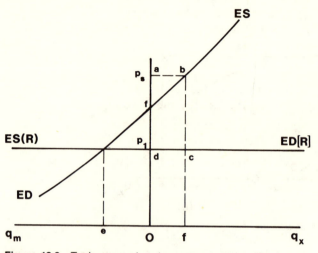

Figure 10.3 Trade reversal and export subsidy

required to move 0*f* onto the international market is *bc*, with total subsidy payments being *abcd*.

If the nation pursuing this kind of trade reversal policy is a large trader in this particular commodity, the relevant portion of *ES(R)-ED(R)* will slope downward to the right. This means that world prices for *q* will be lower for all traders than if the reversal nation were still an importer or even simply self-sufficient. Needless to say, producers and exporting nations around the world who are affected by international prices for *q* are likely to be even more vigorously opposed to this protective policy than if the subsidizing nation were an exporter to begin with.

WELFARE ANALYSIS OF EXPORT SUBSIDIES

In this section we return to the relatively simple concepts of producer and consumer surplus to analyze economic gains and losses caused by an export subsidy. Fig. 10.4 reflects the same basic demand, supply, and price conditions as in Figs. 5.5 and 9.3.

In this particular case, p_1 is the world price and p_2 is the higher, protected internal price. The difference, $p_2 - p_1$, is covered by an export subsidy. Without intervention, 0*c* is produced, *bc* is exported, and 0*b* is consumed domestically. With intervention at p_2, 0*d* is produced and 0*a* is consumed, leaving *ad* to be exported with the subsidy.

This policy increases producer surplus by the area *A + B + C*. In addition, variable inputs are pulled into this sector so that output can expand by the amount *cd*. Output elsewhere in the economy falls by the value of the area under the supply curve between points *c* and *d*. A subsidy is paid on all exports generated at p_2. Its value is *B + C + D*.

Producers gain $A + B + C$, consumers lose $A + B$, and taxpayers distribute $B + C + D$ in export subsidy outlays. The net social losses are areas B and D. Area B is the consumer surplus loss occurring as the amount ab is internally priced at p_2 and exported rather than consumed domestically at p_1. Area D is the part of the treasury payment that covers the extra variable costs of drawing resources into the production of cd. Since the extra output volume cd earns only p_1 on the world market, area D is an efficiency loss to the society. It represents the fall in net value of the economy's output as resources are transferred from elsewhere into subsidized production of q.

PRODUCTION SUBSIDIES AND EXPORTS

Recall that in Chaps. 6 and 7 we examined how deficiency payments and other production subsidies for agricultural products work to shrink imports and protect producers. These schemes tend to be less objectionable to foreign exporters than tariffs or quotas because they have less effect on trade, and they are less visible in the day-to-day operation of markets. Much the same line of argument is appropriate for production subsidies applied by export nations.

Such subsidies are not trade policy schemes in the strict sense, but they may have significant consequences for international trade. Hence, production subsidies are sometimes referred to as implicit export subsidies. We consider two major types of production subsidies that parallel the two export subsidy categories—specific and open-ended.

Specific (or Limited) Production Subsidy

Consider the trade policy implications of a limited production subsidy that is either fixed in its per-unit value or applied as a deliberate, cost-reducing in-

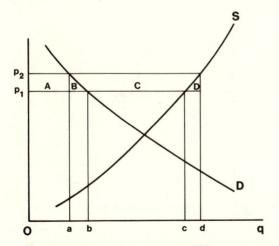

Figure 10.4 Welfare gains and losses from export subsidy

tervention for one or more production inputs, as discussed in Chap. 7. Such a limited subsidy is shown in Fig. 10.5a as a downward shift in the domestic supply function from S to S^*. The vertical displacement of S reflects the per-unit value of the subsidy as it lowers the cost of production and, in turn, the market supply price of the product in question.

This policy-induced change in the domestic supply function leads to a downward shift in the nation's excess supply curve from ES in Fig. 10.5b to ES^*. For a small export nation facing a completely horizontal $ED(R)$ function, as in Fig. 10.5, this intervention causes an expansion in exports of amount cd (Fig. 10.5b). Because the international and domestic market price of q does not change in this case, the export expansion occurs solely because domestic output increases from a to b (Fig. 10.5a). Furthermore, all additional production generated by this subsidy moves onto the export market—ab equals cd.

This cost-reducing production subsidy requires a total government outlay equal to the shaded area in Fig. 10.5a. It is the per-unit value of the subsidy s applied to the now-larger, total production volume. Gross returns to domestic producers expand because of the subsidy-enhanced per-unit value of output (p_1 and s) and larger domestic production. Because the domestic consumption price does not change from p_1, consumers are not punished by this output- and export-expanding policy. However, the society sustains a technical efficiency loss like area D in Fig. 10.4 as output elsewhere in society is sacrificed to expand production behind this subsidy.

The picture alters somewhat if the subsidizing nation is a large exporter, although the fundamental economic reasoning stays much the same. We consider the large-nation case in the following discussion of the open-ended production subsidy. An extension of this illustration back to the specific subsidy case should be clear.

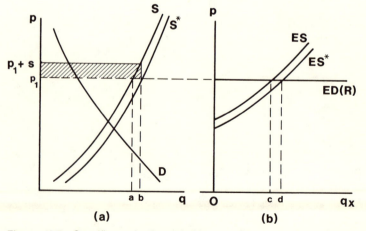

Figure 10.5 Specific production subsidy

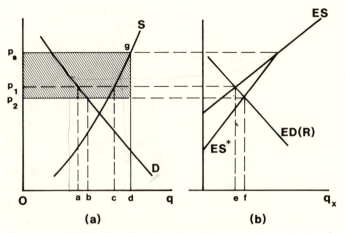

Figure 10.6 Open-ended production subsidy

Open-Ended Subsidy (Deficiency Payments)

Producer price guarantees for export commodities can be sustained by variable production subsidies made as deficiency payments. As with import-competing sectors, deficiency payments are made to producers to cover the difference between the price guarantee and the open-market, international price. In the simple case discussed here, payments are made on all units of domestic output. The open market then allocates the total supply between domestic consumption and exports. As we will see, such a scheme always will expand exports and, in the large-nation case, may increase domestic consumption of the subsidized product.

Consider Fig. 10.6a. The domestic producer price guarantee is fixed at p_s by political action, a mathematical formula, or some other process. If deficiency payments are used to secure this guarantee for farmers, the excess supply ES in Fig. 10.6b is transformed into ES^*. This new excess supply curve is defined by the horizontal difference between the domestic demand D and the vertical line segment gd (up to point g), and then by the difference between D and the domestic supply curve S for possible prices above p_s. Since the producer price guarantee fixes output at point g on the domestic supply curve, the only market adjustment in export volume comes from changes along the domestic demand curve.

This ES^* function is analytically similar to ED^* in the price-guarantee, deficiency-payment scheme of Fig. 6.3. In Fig. 10.6, the slope of ES^* is the same as that of D except it is positive. This is because exports adjust to international prices only to the extent that the amount demanded domestically changes. Supply volume is steady in this illustration because of the fixed producer price guarantee at p_s. Figure 10.6b includes a downward sloping excess demand curve for the rest of the world, reflecting the large-nation assumption for this illustration. The small-nation assumption leads to similar domestic results but involves no international market repercussions.

The free trade, nonintervention price equilibrium is at p_1. When the producer price guarantee at p_s is instituted, ES^* becomes the effective excess supply function. As indicated, world price falls along $ED(R)$ to p_2. Exports increase by the amount ef in Fig. 10.6b. This export increase is the net effect of (1) the expansion in domestic production cd as the producer's price moves up from p_1 to p_s, and (2) the smaller increase in domestic demand volume ab caused by the market price decrease from p_1 to p_2. As long as the $ED(R)$ function is either flat or negatively sloped, exports will expand.

The deficiency payment to producers will be $p_s - p_2$ per unit and will cover all domestic production—$0d$ in this illustration. Total payment outlays are shown as the shaded area in Fig. 10.6a. The larger volume coverage of the deficiency payment compared with an export subsidy is offset in welfare terms by the fact that domestic consumers do not face higher prices because of the trade policy intervention. In fact, with the large-nation case, consumption prices may fall, making buyers of q better off. Taxpayers finance the direct costs of this program, which appear clearly in the national budget.

EXPORT PROMOTION

Public expenditures for export promotion are often part of an expansionary trade philosophy. The objective is to support activities by public officials, trade associations, or private organizations that expand the demand for a nation's export goods, including food and agricultural commodities. Successful demand expansion will translate into larger export volumes, more foreign exchange earnings, and possibly higher domestic prices than otherwise would occur. Such activities are not subsidies or intervention schemes in the ordinary sense, but are elements of a trade policy that tries to bestow advantage on domestic producers.

Activities sponsored as export promotion vary widely. They can include advertising, exhibits, lobbying, and public relations on behalf of a nation's products. They may also involve the exchange of scientific information and experts to improve foreign knowledge about technical aspects of domestically produced items. For export market promotion to be effective, the activities must have at least the potential to expand the amounts demanded from the promoting country. This implies that the nation's promoted products must differ systematically from those of other sellers and/or the exporter is large enough in the world market so that any overall demand expansion created by promotion will increase its own exports.

In analytical terms, these preconditions imply a negatively sloping excess demand function faced by the promoting nation for the products in question. Because promotion activities do not usually involve direct interventions in ordinary commercial transactions, the market price, trade, and welfare implications of export market promotion expenditures remain obscure and problematic. Hence, the arguments for and against such efforts lie beyond the scope of this book, even though they may bulk large in a nation's trade policy.

NONCOMMERCIAL EXPORTS: FOOD AID

Government intervention to sponsor noncommercial food and fiber exports is a relatively common adjunct of agricultural policy in numerous developed nations. Two mutually reinforcing central objectives generally lie behind these undertakings. One is to respond humanely to actual and potential starvation, malnutrition, and related stress in food-short, friendly less-developed countries. The other is to provide a special export outlet for surplus domestic agricultural products that otherwise would press down internal and international prices or would be burdensome to hold as inventory.

In either case, a crucial aspect of truly noncommercial exports is for the commodities to be available under conditions that isolate them from the usual patterns and processes of trade and currency exchange. Noncommercial transfers usually occur as outright gifts, as sales for nonconvertible local currencies, or as credit sales on long-term, special repayment terms. Export (or donor) nations typically wish to avoid international accusations of dumping, export subsidization, and trade disruption for these earmarked shipments. Furthermore, recipient nations typically want to conserve scarce foreign exchange for items not available under special terms. Except in cases of immediate and unforeseen food shortage, noncommercial shipments typically are negotiated either on a multilateral basis or with reasonably open international consultations. Still, disputes about the efficacy, underlying motivation, and spillover effects of noncommercial shipments are common. Like the details of commercial export promotion schemes, these matters lie beyond the scope of this book.

Now let us consider the partial equilibrium economics of two polar cases of noncommercial exports—emergency relief and surplus disposal—both seen from the viewpoint of a large exporter nation. Real-world situations are generally some mixture of these two and typically occur within the complex context of other domestic and trade policies.

Emergency Relief

First imagine that exporter Nation A wishes to respond to either a short-run international food emergency or wishes to carry out a national commitment of food aid for one or more developing countries. The disposal of excess production is not an issue in this instance. Fig. 10.7 gives some insight into the economic effects of such an effort from A's viewpoint.

The government of Nation A undertakes to supply noncommercial exports of, say, powdered milk to an international relief agency or directly to a needy nation. This can be visualized as a rightward shift in domestic demand from D to D^*, the horizontal shift being the volume of powdered milk

committed to the program. The shaded area in Fig. 10.7a is the value of the
government's expenditure for this project.

The impact on the international commercial market is shown in Fig. 10.7b
as *ES* moves to *ES** in response to additional government demand for food
aid supplies. In this large-nation case, the international price moves from p_1
to p_2, causing Nation A's commercial exports to fall as indicated. This occurs
even though domestic production expands from *a* to *b* along *S* and domestic
demand, net of food aid, falls along *D* from *c* to *d*. The government food aid
purchases of *de* more than offset these adjustments, causing a fall in commercial shipments. However, *total* export volume expands from *ca* to *db*.

What is done with this quantity of powdered milk (*de*) is another story
with its own economic and political consequences in the recipient nation.
However, as long as the disposition of this product is fully isolated from the
commercial international market, the direct effects are as indicated in Fig. 10.7.

Surplus Disposal

Next suppose that surplus disposal is the central motivation for an exporter's
noncommercial shipments. Fig. 10.8 illustrates how such a program might unfold. Imagine that exporter Nation B wishes to maintain its domestic prices
of wheat at p_1. However, the systematic adoption of new production
technology has moved the partial equilibrium domestic supply curve relentlessly
from *S* to *S**. In the absence of intervention, Nation B's excess supply curve
would shift from *ES* to *ES**, pushing domestic and world prices below p_1. The
equilibrium shown at point *a* Fig. 10.8a indicates this potential effect.

Now suppose that the government of Nation B responds by taking the
volume *de* in Fig. 10.8a off the domestic wheat market via direct purchases
or other official acquisitions. (Note that *de* in Fig.10.8a is equal to *bc* in Fig.

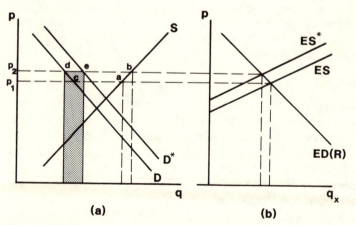

(a)   **(b)**

Figure 10.7   Emergency relief food aid

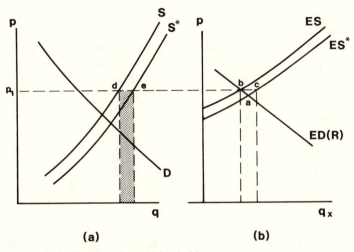

Figure 10.8 Surplus disposal food aid

10.8*b*). Wheat prices will remain at p_1. Volumes moving in the commercial and domestic markets will not change as a result of this program. Hence, total export volume will expand if *de* is shipped abroad. Government expenditures in Nation B for price support via these acquisitions are indicated by the shaded area in Fig. 10.8*a*. The wheat thus obtained is available for transfer to recipient nations as noncommercial aid. However, the primary motivation for acquisition in this case was price support.

As an aside to this international food aid discussion, we note that there is nothing inherent in this description or analysis that necessarily restricts the disposition of the commodities to foreign recipients. Part or all of the milk or wheat acquired by the governments could be used for noncommercial distribution to disadvantaged individuals and groups within Nations A and B. The price and trade impacts would be the same as indicated as long as the use of the supplies was insulated from and additional to ordinary commercial transactions.

SUMMARY

Nations pursuing an expansionary export trade policy are sometimes accused of dumping on international markets. Dumping occurs when goods are sold abroad at less than their production costs or at prices lower than those prevailing in domestic markets. Export and production subsidies cause exports to be larger than they otherwise would be and typically generate internal prices and/or production costs that are higher than comparable values on international markets.

As with most trade policy intervention schemes, there are net social losses and redistributions of economic value within any society providing

export-expanding subsidies. Export promotion activities financed with public
funds attempt to shift the excess demand for a nation's exports outward sufficiently far enough to generate significant increases in export volume and possibly
prices. Food aid exports on noncommercial terms provide additional foreign
outlets for products acquired by governments either directly for relief assistance
or as an adjunct of domestic price-support operations.

QUESTIONS

10.3 Assume you are an economic adviser to the minister of trade for the nation of
Westonia. The minister wishes to know the general trade, price, and economic
welfare effects of a fixed-price guarantee for Westonian butter producers. Westonia
is a large butter exporter to the world market. The price guarantee in this case
is to be sustained by deficiency payments, not a direct export subsidy. Advise
the minister.

10.2 You are still advising the Westonian minister of trade. The problem now is to
assess the economic effects, including welfare aspects, of shifting from a deficiency payments scheme to an export subsidy on butter in order to maintain a
fixed producer-price guarantee. Advise the minister.

10.3 The Westonian Dairy Promotion Board is a private organization of diary farmers
and related interests. The board argues vigorously that a butter export subsidy
will bring about undesirable side effects, including trade policy retaliation by importers and other butter exporters. They propose, instead, a publicly financed
promotion campaign (managed by the board) that would expand exports sufficiently so that no other policy intervention would be needed to maintain the
original producer-price guarantee. Discuss the partial equilibrium economics of
this proposal, including the demand expansion that would be required for this
proposal to be successful. How large a promotion budget could be justified?

10.4 Industria has decided to subsidize its exports of plywood to all buyers. The subsidy S is to be calculated according to the following formula: $S = 1/(p_w + k)$,
where p_w is the world price of plywood and k is a fixed number. Illustrate this
particular subsidy policy using partial equilibrium supply and demand relations.
Discuss its economic implications for Industria, including the timber industry.

ADDITIONAL READINGS

Corden, W. M. 1971. *The Theory of Protection,* Clarendon Press, Oxford, England,
pp. 14–27. (Protection of exportables is covered here, including export subsidies,
production subsidies, and trade reversal.)

Greenaway, D. 1983. *Trade Policy and the New Protectionism,* St. Martin's Press, New
York, New York, pp. 146–147. (A short, partial equilibrium analysis of export
subsidies.)

Grennes, T. 1984. *International Economics,* Prentice-Hall, Englewood Cliffs, New Jersey,
pp. 179–181 and 317–318. (These two short passages focus on export subsidies and
food aid respectively.)

Hartland-Thunberg, P. and Crawford, M. H. 1982. *Government Support for Exports,*
Lexington Books, Lexington, Massachusetts. (An entire book devoted to export

subsidies with a United States focus; see especially Chaps. 1 and 2.)

Hufbauer, G. C. and Erb, J. S. 1984. *Subsidies in International Trade,* MIT Press, Cambridge, Massachusetts. (A whole book about export subsidies with an international focus; see especially Chap. 3.)

Krauss, M. B. 1978. *The New Protectionism,* New York University Press, New York, pp. 68–91. (A discussion, including some analysis, of dumping, production subsidies, and export subsidies.)

Michaely, M. 1977. *Theory of Commercial Policy,* University of Chicago Press, Chicago, Illinois, pp. 51–54. (A general equilibrium discussion of export subsidies using diagrams.)

Paarlberg, P. L. 1984. "When Are Export Subsidies Rational?" *Agricultural Economics Research,* 36(1):1–7, Economic Research Service, U.S. Department of Agriculture, Washington, D.C. (A relatively rigorous partial equilibrium discussion of export subsidies with diagrams and some mathematics.)

Sorenson, V. L. 1975. *International Trade Policy: Agriculture and Development,* Michigan State University International and Business Studies, East Lansing, Michigan, pp. 115–117. (A short discussion of food aid exports.)

Chapter 11

Market and Price Discrimination

Several agricultural export nations, especially those exporting grains and oilseeds, use some form of market or price discrimination to enhance total returns to growers. Market discrimination schemes have a long tradition in the organization of both domestic and international marketing. Other common terms for essentially similar ideas are "two-price" and "multiple-price" plans. Another term dating back to the 1930s is "market prorates."

The fundamental idea behind these schemes is that the buyers of a product may be separated into two or more groups that are clearly distinguishable from each other. If the product, whatever it is, cannot be traded or arbitraged between these separate groups, different prices for it can be charged within each group. If demand response to price (elasticity) differs among the groups, total returns for producers can be enhanced beyond amounts generated when fully open markets and free trade prevail. For this possibility to be exploited, it is also necessary that there be some centralized monopoly authority that has both the power and ability to control the distribution of the total supplies into each separate market.

Classic applications of agricultural market and price discrimination include fluid versus processed milk utilization, fresh versus processed fruit and vegetable utilization, brand name versus private label distribution of similar food products and, of course, domestic versus export market sales. Although the same fundamental principles apply to all these cases, we will focus on the last. Natural and political boundaries between nations provide clear market demarcations that usually can be sustained by the exporter against backflow and arbitrage. Because the international market is generally larger in total than the domestic market, demand responsiveness to price can be expected to differ systematically between domestic and international sales. Finally, numerous countries have statutory marketing boards or government monopolies with sufficient authority and ability to control the distribution of products between the home and international markets. This is especially true in the international grain market.

We will probe the basic economics of export market discrimination in a two-part sequence of ideas. First, we will consider the consequences of discriminatory allocation of a fixed supply volume between two separate markets. Then we will discuss how enhanced returns from discrimination can be distributed among producers and how this distribution, in turn, affects output supply response and resource allocation.

MARKET DISCRIMINATION WITH A FIXED SUPPLY

Imagine that Nation A is a grain exporter with a sizable domestic market. Annually, a fixed amount of grain $\bar{q}$ is to be distributed between the home market q_h and the export market q_x. If all the previously discussed market conditions are met, total returns from the sale of q can be enhanced beyond those obtainable from the free market. To do this, additional q must be allocated to the more price-elastic market and less allocated to the less price-elastic market by Nation A's grain marketing board. On the plausible assumption that the smaller domestic market is less price-elastic than the potentially larger world market, this means shorting the domestic market and sending more into the export market than otherwise would be the case. This is the predominant pattern of behavior with such schemes in the real world.

Fig. 11.1 is one way to illustrate the basic partial equilibrium economics of this problem. The amount allocated to the home market is measured from point a to the right along the horizontal axis. The amount allocated to the export market is measured to the left from point c. The full distance ac is equal to $\bar{q}$, which is the fixed supply of grain to be allocated.

Domestic demand in Nation A is the curve labeled D_h. It is drawn in relation to the origin at point a. Export demand is D_x, drawn in relation to the origin at point c. If q can flow freely between the export and domestic markets, the price p_o will prevail in both, with amount ad being consumed domestically and amount cd being exported.

Let the marginal revenue curves for the two markets be denoted by M_h and M_x respectively. Marginal revenue is the addition to total revenue caused by a one-unit increase in sales to a particular market. Marginal revenue curves, therefore, are schedules of additional revenues associated with each unit of volume. At the free market position with one price (p_o) ruling, the marginal revenue in the export market is higher than the corresponding marginal revenue

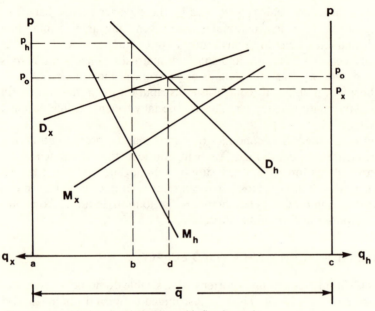

Figure 11.1 Market discrimination with fixed supply

in the home market. This phenomenon occurs because, at least in this neighborhood, the domestic demand curve is less price responsive (elastic) than the export demand curve. Readers who are not familiar with the relationship between marginal revenue curves and demand functions can consult virtually any modern textbook in microeconomics. For instance, the small-nation assumption for the exporter will result in a perfectly horizontal D_x function. In this case, D_x and M_x are identical. The rest of the argument is the same as the case illustrated in Fig. 11.1.

Aggregate revenue obtainable from a fixed $\bar{q}$ can be increased by the board's moving one unit from the less-elastic home market into the more-elastic export market. This maneuver would move the market allocation point in Fig. 11.1 slightly to the left of d. Successive reallocations from the home market to the export market will continue to enhance total revenue until the allocation indicated by point b is reached. Here, the marginal revenue in each market is equal. Further quantity adjustments in either direction by the board will not increase aggregate revenue.

At this position, the price in the home market of Nation A will be p_h and the price in the export market will be p_x (Fig. 11.1). This typical market discrimination scheme raises the home price, possibly lowers the world price, and increases total returns to sellers. A complete formal analysis of this scheme would involve further theoretical possibilities. For example, we could consider whether or not both marginal revenues become negative in the relevant range and whether or not costless disposal of q is possible.

No matter what the particulars, the fundamental economic argument and its line of reasoning are not really changed. Total producer revenue is maximized when marginal revenues are equal in each market. But whether or not this maximum is achieved, it is true that total returns are increased by allocating sales from a point like *d* toward a point like *b*. As with other exporter schemes that increase domestic market prices, some form of binding import controls must be in place to prevent the domestic market from being inundated from abroad.

Market discrimination of this kind with a fixed quantity uses unequal market prices to redistribute economic value away from domestic consumers toward domestic producers. This value redistribution is either enhanced or slightly offset as export sales are increased, depending on the price elasticity in the export market. In either case, foreign buyers may benefit if lower international prices occur.

DISTRIBUTION OF REVENUE AND SUPPLY RESPONSE

Any agency or board administering a multiple-price, market-discrimination scheme also faces the problem of how to distribute revenues to domestic producers who, we will assume, are numerous. This is generally quite realistic in agricultural applications. Since two or more selling prices exist for the board, there is no single, clear-cut way to approach this task. Yet, how this disbursement is managed has an important effect on the supply response of producers and therefore on the subsequent operation of the scheme.

Two main approaches have been employed for agricultural products. One is to pool the aggregate proceeds of all sales from domestic and foreign markets, subtract operating expenses, then pay producers a weighted-average or blend price for each unit marketed. The other is to disburse the higher domestic returns among eligible producers according to some prearranged formula. Entitlement to these higher returns might be based on previous production or sales records for some base period. Any other arbitrary principle could be employed. For individual marketings in excess of this initial entitlement (or quota), a lower price, based on per-unit earnings in the world market, is paid.

It also would be clearly possible for the board to keep all or part of the discrimination proceeds as government revenue, returning only the world price (or less) to producers. However, we will not pursue the consequences of this taxation method here. In addition, we will not expressly investigate production or marketing limitations that might be applied to individual sellers who are covered by a discrimination scheme.

The reason the two major disbursement approaches differ in their supply response effects is that they differ in the way producers are paid for their final (marginal) units of output. Economic principles tell us that individual decisions to expand or contract farm production are based on how marginal revenue earned (or foregone) from one more (or less) unit of output compares with the marginal cost of producing it. With the pooled or blend-price approach, the individual producer's marginal revenue is a weighted average of the higher domestic price and the lower world price. This blend value will be higher than the comparable marginal revenue in the entitlement situation because, in the latter instance, marginal revenue for additional output is essentially the world price or its equivalent.

Continuing with our grain exporter example, we can illustrate this distinction in Fig. 11.2 for a representative grain producer i in Nation A. A positively sloping marginal cost function for this producer is represented by MC_i. This function is the added cost of producing one more unit of grain at each output quantity. On the vertical axis, p_W is the world price, p_D is the higher domestic price sustained through import controls and market discrimination by the grain marketing board, and p_B is a blend price average of p_W and p_D. The larger the ratio of export sales to domestic sales, the closer p_B will be to p_W. On the horizontal axis, $0c$ is the proportional, prorated entitlement of the domestic market held by producer i.

Under the entitlement or quota approach, this producer receives the amount $hac0$ from the board for the domestically sold portion of output and $bfdc$ based on the per-unit value of p_W for everything else. Here, p_W is the producer's marginal revenue. In principle, the producer will equate that value with marginal cost, producing a total output of $0d$. In this case, the marginal value obtained from the international market on the last unit of output is equal to the marginal domestic cost of obtaining it—at point f. Hence, productive resources will be efficiently allocated at the margin no matter what other welfare and redistributional consequences occur in the domestic economy because of the higher, discriminating domestic price.

The blend-price situation generates a different result. Since p_B is higher than p_W, an individual grain producer receiving the blend price will equate marginal revenue and marginal cost at point g. This generates the larger grain

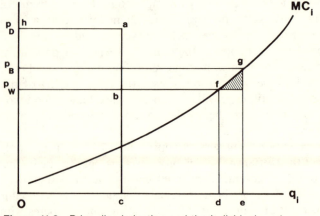

Figure 11.2 Price discrimination and the individual producer

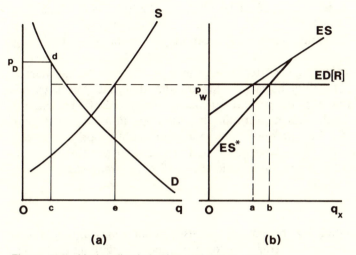

Figure 11.3 Market discrimination and export supply

output $0e$. Each output unit beyond d is sold at the world price p_W, but each costs an incrementally higher amount. The shaded area in Fig. 11.2 represents for the individual producer the value lost to the broader economy caused by producing de units of grain and selling them at p_W. An aggregation of these shaded areas over all grain producers is a partial equilibrium measure of the total social resource cost of the discrimination program when a blend price is employed. This total value corresponds to area D in the welfare analysis of Fig. 10.4.

Both approaches to producer payment with market discrimination lead to more exports than with free trade. However, the blend-price approach is the more expansionary of the two. Consider Fig. 11.3, which reflects domestic and international markets for a small country producing and exporting q under a simple market discrimination plan. The domestic consumption price is fixed at p_D. This price may or may not equate marginal revenues between home and export sales—it is simply higher than the international price. Once p_D is established, the ordinary ES function in Fig. 11.3b converts to ES^*. In this case, ES^* is the horizontal difference between S and the vertical line dc in Fig. 11.3a. Note that $0c$ is the domestic quantity demanded at p_D.

The new ES^* function lies to the right of ES because no domestic consumption response will occur as world prices increase or decrease as long as they are below p_D. When the market discriminating board employs a producer payment scheme based on p_W for output beyond $0c$, exports are $0b$ in Fig. 11.3b rather than the free market volume of $0a$. The higher domestic price shrinks internal use below free market consumption. This amount must then be exported by the board.

It is not easy to illustrate the blend-price case with simple diagrams since that price is a complex function of p_D, p_W, domestic consumption, and total output. But we can see that in reference to Fig. 11.3 the equilibrium blend price will lie above p_W but below p_D. This blend price will generate more output than $0e$ in Fig. 11.3a and therefore more exports than either $0a$ or $0b$ in Fig. 11.3b.

If the discriminating exporter is large in relation to the world market, $ED(R)$ of Fig. 11.3b will be negatively sloped rather than flat. A little experimentation will show that the general conclusions suggested by Fig. 11.2 and 11.3 still remain valid. Market discrimination will result in more exports than free trade no matter how producers are paid, with the blend-price approach yielding more exports. In the large export nation case, these additional exports will tend to press the international price below the free trade value.

SUMMARY

Market discrimination is a trade policy tool used by some agricultural exporting nations to enhance total returns to domestic producers without explicit export or production subsidies. A central authority or board with monopoly power allocates domestic supplies to increase volume sold in the more price-elastic export markets. As long as the two (or more) markets can be kept separate, total returns from sales, via the board, may be enhanced. Economic value is transferred from domestic consumers to domestic producers and export earnings are expanded.

Discrimination schemes of this kind generally result in more exports than otherwise would occur. In addition, total output in the discriminating export nation may expand to an economically inefficient volume if per-unit returns to producers at the margin are based on a pooled average of domestic and international prices.

QUESTIONS

11.1 The country of Rindland is a large exporter of citrus fruit. The national Citrus Marketing Board controls the purchase and sales of all citrus produced in Rindland. The board is trying to decide if and how to allocate each season's production among four outlets—fresh and processed for domestic consumption and fresh and processed for export. The board's goal is to enhance grower returns if possible. Can it be done? How?

11.2 Suppose that the Rindland Citrus Marketing Board paid its individual growers prices based on pooled returns from all sales—domestic, foreign, fresh, and processed. Assess the long-run economic implications of this policy on production, prices, and economic efficiency.

11.3 The Wheat Marketing Board of Heartland, a large exporter, has been buying wheat domestically at p_s and selling it abroad at the lower world price of p_W. The board recently decided to use its domestic monopoly power to discriminate between the less-elastic home market and the more-elastic export market. It decided to continue to pay producers p_s, but now as a blend price. Illustrate and discuss the price, production, export, and domestic consumption aspects of this policy shift.

11.4 Suppose that the marginal revenue curves M_h and M_x of Fig. 11.1 had crossed each other *below* the horizontal axis rather than above it. Discuss the economic circumstances that could lead to such an occurrence. What would a sensible marketing board do in this case if its objective was to maximize producer returns from the fixed supply of $\bar{q}$?

ADDITIONAL READINGS

Bressler, R. G. and King, R. A. 1970. *Markets, Prices, and Interregional Trade,* John Wiley & Sons, New York, New York, Chap. 12. (A thorough discussion of price discrimination in a U.S. agricultural context.)

Campbell, K. O. 1973. *Agricultural Marketing and Prices,* Cheshire Publishing, Melbourne, Australia. (Chaps. 7 and 8 especially. This text focuses on agriculture and policy in Australia, a country that has a long tradition of employing market and price discrimination schemes.)

Dahl, D. C. and Hammond, J. W. 1977. *Market and Price Analysis: The Agricultural Industries,* McGraw-Hill, New York, New York. (Price discrimination economics, including the blend-price issue.)

Phlips, L. 1983. *Economics of Price Discrimination.* Cambridge University Press, New York, New York. (As the title suggests, this is a whole book on the topic; some of it is rather rigorous economic theory and some is quite readable. The author argues that almost all real-world prices are discriminatory, hence the topical coverage is broad.)

Throsby, C. D. (ed.) 1972. *Agricultural Policy,* Penguin Books, Middlesex, England, Chap. 17. (This chapter is a paper by R. M. Parish that discusses the Australian dairy program, especially the market discrimination and price pooling economics of this scheme.)

Tomek, W. G. and Robinson, K. L. 1981. *Agricultural Product Prices,* 2nd ed., Cornell University Press, Ithaca, New York, pp. 107–115. (A short, clear treatment of price discrimination economics.)

Waugh, F. V. 1984. *Selected Writings on Agricultural Policy and Economic Analysis* (J. P. Houck and M. E. Abel, eds.), University of Minnesota Press, Minneapolis, Minnesota, pp. 107–126 and 132–145. (These two papers are classical discussions of price discrimination by a pioneer in the application of these ideas to agricultural products.)

Chapter 12

Export Taxes, Controls, and Embargoes

Export trade policy is not always devoted to the expansion of international sales or the protection of producers. Governments frequently implement policy schemes that reduce export marketings of particular commodities to protect domestic buyers and users and/or to raise revenue for the national treasury. In addition, governments occasionally cut off or restrict exports to specific nations for foreign policy or other political reasons. The major tools employed for these purposes are either export taxes or direct, quantitative controls. These interventions are the subject of this chapter.

EXPORT TAXES

Export taxes are levies applied as products leave a nation on their way to foreign destinations. They are a mirror image of import tariffs. Hence, export taxes may be fixed per-unit levies, ad valorem duties, or some combination of the two. Like tariffs, they place an economic wedge between international and domestic prices. With export taxes, domestic prices are pushed below international prices. This reverses the situation with import tariffs, which elevate domestic prices above international prices.

Export taxes may be levied by governments for two main reasons. One is to deliberately depress domestic prices to protect internal buyers or consumers of the exported product from having to pay higher international prices. The other reason is to generate revenue for the central authority. Both effects occur when an export tax is levied, but usually one is the dominant motive. The following illustrations emphasize and explore these dual aspects of an export tax. Both the small- and large-nation cases are discussed.

Protection for Domestic Buyers

First consider an export tax designed principally to protect domestic consumers from eager foreign buyers. Such a tax might be levied by a low-income nation on its exports of a crucial staple food product like rice, wheat, or vegetable oil. The economic and political aspects of such an export tax indicate that the government wishes to protect consumers (most likely low-income urban wage earners and unemployed people) at the expense of domestic farmers, export merchants, its own foreign exchange earnings, and foreign buyers. At the same time, the taxing government receives a bonus of some additional tax revenue.

To illustrate, consider a small exporting country, Nation C, facing what it regards as a fixed world price for rice, an important domestic staple product. Since our attention is still on the export side, we draw the excess supply curve ES of Nation C in the right quadrant of Fig. 12.1b. With no trade policy intervention by the government, the horizontal excess demand curve for the rest of the trading world $ED(R)$ determines the domestic rice price p_1. At this price, domestic consumption is ab, domestic production is ac, and exports are bc. The same volume of exports is indicated as df in Fig. 12.1b.

Now suppose Nation C decides to levy an ad valorem export tax on rice. This decision generates ES^* in Fig. 12.1b. This function lies above ES by the per-unit value of the tax T at each volume of exports. Hence, ES^* is the tax-burdened supply function for rice of Nation C faced by the rest of the world. In this particular example, T is not a fixed per-unit value. As an ad valorem tax, it increases as the international market price increases and decreases as that price falls.

The establishment of this export tax presses the domestic rice price down to p_2. This occurs as rice exporters, having to pay the tax, reduce their commitments and additional domestic supplies are pushed onto internal markets. The difference between p_1 and p_2 is the equilibrium per-unit value of the export tax. As the domestic rice price falls, buyers benefit. They obtain more of this important food commodity at a lower price along D. Domestic consumption increases from ab to gh.

However, the lower domestic price punishes local rice producers in Nation C. Instead of earning higher world prices, they obtain lower prices and therefore reduce output to gj, along S, leaving a smaller volume hj to be exported. In Fig. 12.1b, this smaller export volume is indicated as kl. Although the export tax reduces domestic production and exports, it will generate some revenue for Nation C's central authority as an incidental consequence of the lower internal prices. This revenue is indicated by the shaded area in Fig. 12.1a and by $delk$ in Fig. 12.1b. This area is the per-unit value of the export tax multiplied by the now tax-burdened volume of rice exports.

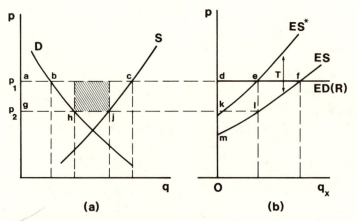

Figure 12.1   Ad valorem export tax to protect domestic consumers

Generating Tax Revenue

Export taxes have a long history of use by primary-product or raw-material exporting nations as a way to secure revenue for the central government. In nations where there are long-standing political and organizational impediments to collecting income, excise, and other taxes, export levies are an attractive taxation mechanism. They do place a burden on domestic producers of the taxed commodity by pushing down their prices, but for some governments it may be the only feasible way to tax such producers and/or their output.

Imagine that a major banana-exporting country, Nation E, levies a fixed per-unit tax on outward-bound shipments mainly to generate government revenue. Assume that domestic banana consumption is very small relative to production and exports, so the protection of domestic users is not a major concern. However, E's exports are large in relation to the world's banana market. Figure 12.2 depicts this case. Domestic demand D is small relative to supply S, making ES in Fig. 12.2b almost the same as S in Fig. 12.2a. The free trade equilibrium is determined by the intersection of ES with the negatively sloped excess demand curve $ED(R)$ for the rest of the world. In this setting, the free trade domestic and international banana price is p_1. Domestic production is ac and the small domestic banana consumption is ab. Hence, bc or its equivalent, df, are exports.

Now imagine that Nation E's government places a fixed per-unit export tax on banana shipments. This creates the tax-burdened excess supply curve ES^* in Fig. 12.2b. The vertical difference between ES^* and ES is the export tax T. Operating against the negatively sloping $ED(R)$ function, this export tax levy pushes up international prices to p_3, but depresses domestic prices to p_2. The impact on domestic banana production and exports is negative, as before, but the shaded area *jegh* in Fig. 12.2b is captured by the government as tax revenue.

Export Taxation by a Monopoly Board

As with import tariffs and quotas, the same economic results and revenues would occur if instead of levying an export tax a government agency or board exercised monopoly export authority over E's banana trade. This agency could buy bananas from domestic producers at p_2 and sell on international markets at p_3. The per-unit difference T and the shaded area *jegh* would be government revenue, but private exporters would not be involved and a specific export tax would not be collected as such.

When a large nation imposes an export tax, international prices tend to increase as exports fall, from p_1 to p_3 in Fig. 12.2. These price increases benefit competitive producers and punish consumers in other countries if the prices they face are linked to those in world markets.

A Prohibitive Export Tax

Just as there is some tariff amount that will choke off all imports, there is also an export tax rate that will choke off all exports. Consider sequential increases in the export tax T in Fig. 12.1. The excess supply curve faced by foreigners, ES^*, will move to successively higher and leftward positions. Exports will fall until the per-unit tax reaches the difference between the world price at d and the isolation equilibrium price at m. At that point, exports are zero, no revenue is generated, and further export tax increases will have no effect. In terms of the specific commodity example, Nation C, by applying a prohibitive export tax, could achieve autarky in the production and consumption of rice, but at lower prices than would otherwise prevail.

Export Tax Revenue

Consider a very small export tax that is gradually increased. As the per-unit levy grows in size, taxed exports will fall. Revenue will increase, reach a maximum, then fall. If both the ES and $ED(R)$ functions are straight lines, it is

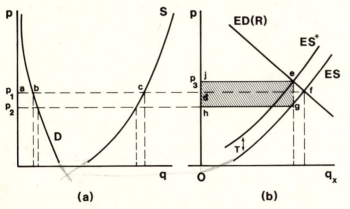

Figure 12.2 A fixed export tax to generate government revenue

true that maximum export tax earnings occur when exports are exactly one-half their free trade amount. This parallels the Chap. 5 argument about maximum import tariff revenues.

Other shapes for *ES* and *ED(R)* will yield other results, but there is always a maximum revenue export-tax position somewhere between zero and the free trade export volume. In the small-nation case, for instance, the maximum export-tax revenue occurs when the ratio of the domestic price to the per-unit tax is exactly equal to the positive value of the price elasticity of the exporting nation's excess supply function.

Gains, Losses, and Welfare Analysis

With export taxes generally, the direct losers are domestic producers and possibly foreign buyers. In addition, firms and individuals involved in handling export quantities and supplying production inputs also tend to lose because output and export volume are generally reduced with an export tax.

Unless the excess demand function for the taxed export is highly price inelastic, the foreign exchange earnings for the nation will be lower than otherwise. The steeper the domestic supply function, the smaller the foreign exchange earnings loss. All these losses can be viewed as the economic costs of obtaining tax revenue for the government's benefit or of keeping consumer prices lower than they otherwise would be. Hence, the gainers from an export tax are domestic consumers, the tax-levying government, and possibly foreign sellers.

Let us use partial equilibrium consumer and producer surplus ideas to analyze economic gains and losses for the domestic economy from the imposition of an export tax. The gains and losses are, as might be expected, a mirror image of the welfare effects of the import tariff or quota.

Consider Fig. 12.3. Its underlying assumptions and interpretation are much the same as those of Figs. 5.5 and 10.4. At the free trade price p_1, this nation is an exporter of q, exporting a volume of *ad* units. Domestic production is $0d$ and domestic consumption is $0a$. The export tax in this simple case lowers the domestic price to p_2, increasing domestic consumption by *ab* but decreasing production by *cd*. Thus, exports fall to *bc*.

This policy maneuver reduces producer surplus by the value $A + B + C + D$. Variable inputs in this illustration move into other competitive uses, but the fixed inputs in the q sector earn rewards that are lower than with free trade. This fall is a loss of producer surplus.

How does this producer surplus loss spread throughout the economy? The value A becomes an increase in consumer surplus because of the fall in price from p_1 to p_2. The value C is picked up as tax revenue to the government, collected on exports of *bc*. This leaves the triangles B and D to be accounted for.

These values, B and D, are "losses" to the society much the same as similar triangles are losses in the tariff case. The area D represents a net loss because *cd* units of q that could be sold for p_1 are not produced after the tax is im-

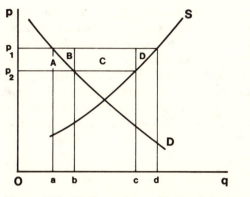

Figure 12.3 Welfare gains and losses from export tax

posed. The released variable inputs move into successively lower-valued activities elsewhere in the economy. The area B also is a loss to the society. It is the producer surplus lost because the quantity ab is sold to domestic buyers at p_2 rather than to foreign buyers at p_1. It is a net loss after considering the gain in consumer surplus, area A. So in the partial equilibrium context, areas B and D are net costs to society of protecting consumers from higher international prices and of being able to generate government revenue from an export tax.

Optimal Export Tax

In the same way that a large importing nation can select an optimal tariff (Chap. 5), a large exporting nation can, in principle, select an optimal export tax. The idea here is that the exporter, by driving up international prices, can obtain tax revenues sufficient to offset its social losses—areas B and D in Fig. 12.3—and possibly have something left over. The complete theory of the optimal export tax is not outlined here but involves rules for selecting the tax rate that maximizes the difference between tax revenues generated and social losses caused by its imposition. As with the tariff side, the optimal export tax is lower than the maximum-revenue export tax.

EXPORT CONTROLS AND EMBARGOES

Sometimes an exporting nation may decide to control directly the quantities of one or more of its products entering international markets. These quantitative trade restrictions may be general, applying to all potential export destinations, or they may be directed specifically against purchases by particular import nations.

General export controls typically are invoked to protect domestic consumers from all eager foreign buyers. Export restrictions pointed at particular customers often are called embargoes, and are usually invoked for political or strategic reasons. They may or may not be effective in economic terms. We will consider both types of export controls in this section.

Because agricultural products, particularly food and feed grains, are regarded by most nations as strategic goods for national security, the control of this export by governments of surplus-producing nations is a matter of substantial trade policy interest. Both economic and political motives intertwine in the analysis of export controls and embargoes. Our discussion here will emphasize the economic implications.

Analytical Framework

Whatever their objectives, export controls are the analytical counterpart of import quotas. The economic impacts and welfare results of general export controls are virtually the same as with export taxes. For illustration, let us consider a large wheat-exporting nation. Imagine that in order to maintain a lower domestic wheat price this nation decides to limit the total export quantities in each crop year. For this control to be effective (binding), it must reduce exports below amounts that would otherwise have been shipped. In Fig. 12.4b, let that controlled amount be $\bar{q}_x$.

The volume $\bar{q}_x$ is a binding export quota on wheat because it is less than the amount exported in the free trade situation (point a in Fig. 12.4b). Following our previous diagram conventions, we identify ES^* as the excess supply curve faced by buyers in the international market. The intersection of ES^* and the world's excess demand curve $ED(R)$ produces an equilibrium solution for world wheat trade d, at which p_3 is the new, higher world price. The international price increases because the world wheat market is shorted by the binding export quota. On the other hand, the bottling up of unexported wheat on the domestic market produces a lower internal price equilibrium at b. Supplies are pushed back into the domestic economy where wheat consumption expands but production falls. This is familiar ground. It follows the export tax story.

The export control causes a wedge to open between international and domestic wheat prices whether or not the controlling exporter bulks large on the world market. The special impact of a large nation in this setting is to cause an elevation in the world price. The wedge between lower domestic prices and higher world prices means that there are windfall gains for those who obtain the scarce rights to export wheat. These gains, $edbc$ in Fig. 12.4b, are rents to these scarce exporting rights. The questions of who earns these rents and how quota amounts are allocated among economic agents are exactly the same as with binding import quotas. If the exports of wheat, for instance, are totally in the hands of a government agency or a monopoly marketing board, export control rents accrue directly and fully to that body as it buys at low internal prices and sells abroad at higher rates.

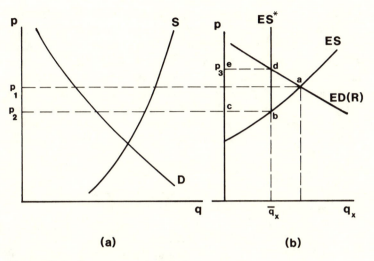

Figure 12.4 General export controls

The more stringent the export controls relative to open market exports, the lower the internal price and, in the large-nation case, the higher the international price. Also, the more stringent the controls, the larger the per-unit rent value of the export quotas. Export controls by a large trading nation punish all foreign buyers with higher international prices but give an advantage to all competing foreign sellers who are influenced by international prices.

Export Controls as a Short-Run Measure

Agricultural export quotas or controls can be, and often have been, used as an immediate short-run response to unexpected domestic food shortages, sudden surges in export demand caused perhaps by crop failures elsewhere, or a combination of both. In such situations, the short-run objective is to insulate domestic food buyers, at least temporarily, from rapid price increases and possible supply shortages. These ideas are illustrated in Fig. 12.5 for one particular example.

Suppose that Nation E initially is following a free trade policy in its exports of raw cotton. The free trade equilibrium point is indicated by a in Fig. 12.5b, with p_1 being both the international and domestic price. Imagine that an unexpected shift to the left in the domestic cotton supply function from S_1 to S_2 occurs as a result of a serious crop failure in Nation E. At the same time, suppose that the foreign cotton demand shifts to the right from $ED(R)_1$ to $ED(R)_2$ either because competing foreign supplies also are momentarily scarce or because foreign textile demand suddenly increases.

In this illustration, the free trade equilibrium would move to point b. This involves a sizable price jump from p_1 to p_2 and no change in export volume. All adjustments to the short supply would be forced on cotton users in Nation

E as prices escalate from p_1 to p_2 and consumption falls along D. Internal political pressure might cause E's government to invoke general export controls on cotton to combat the free trade price increase. Suppose the government clamps on export controls sufficiently tight that the domestic cotton price of p_1 is maintained. The new, controlled excess supply function is ES_2^*. It maintains the previous internal price but shorts the world market of cotton shipments. Then price p_3 occurs in the international trading arena as raw cotton becomes scarce. Quota rents of $p_3 - p_1$ per unit are available inside Nation E to individuals or firms with access to export privileges under the controls.

Export Embargoes

Occasionally, governments are motivated to embargo agricultural (or other) exports to only one or a few potential customer nations. The term "embargo" denotes a legal restriction against shipments to specific destinations. Such embargoes have their roots in political disagreements, strategic international maneuvers that somehow override usual economic considerations, or actual military conflict.

The analytical framework we have been using to discuss various trade policy schemes is not really useful for a country-specific export embargo. Implicit in our diagrams and discussion is that the commodity under consideration, or a close substitute for it, is or can be produced readily in other trading nations and that international arbitrage, resale, and transshipment are possible. In such cases, a country-specific export embargo could have no major, lasting effects on either the nation at which it was directed or other countries across the trading world.

To be sure, the sudden application of a country-specific trade embargo would likely disrupt world markets until new trading arrangements and patterns were formed to accommodate the restriction's political dimensions. The

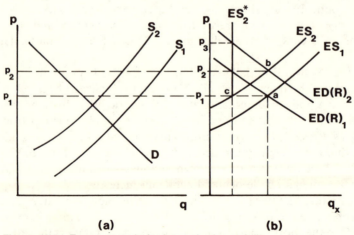

Figure 12.5 Export controls for internal price stability

short-term commercial disruptions and uncertainties created as a government embargo cuts across prior business agreements, commitments, and contracts are not to be minimized. However, they are not easy to build into our relatively simple economic framework. We can argue that if preembargo trade patterns were relatively efficient, considering both transportation and transaction costs, the new, postembargo patterns might be less efficient from a technical standpoint. This inefficiency would create slightly lower prices for the embargoing nation and slightly higher prices for everyone else, including the target nation.

For a narrowly focused export embargo to be effective against one or a few target countries, two quite stringent conditions must be met:

1 The embargoing nation must have a monopoly or near-monopoly on the world's production of the product in question, or it must convince all other potential suppliers of this product not to expand their sales to the embargoed nation.

2 Transshipment of embargoed products through third countries or intermediaries to the target nation is not possible or is prevented.

In the absence of offsetting government actions at home, any export control scheme, including an effective embargo, will generate lower domestic prices. Naturally, lower prices benefit domestic buyers and hurt domestic sellers. In addition, the total volume of exports is curtailed.

If the stringent conditions for success fully hold, sealing off one importer will not affect international prices if the volume previously exported to the embargoed nation is held entirely off the world market. In this case, export quota rents will develop in the embargoing nation as its internal price falls and access to the remaining international export market becomes limited.

On the other hand, if the embargoing nation does nothing to control its export volume, world prices will fall and quota or access rents may emerge for individuals (wherever they are) who, under the terms of the embargo, retain the ability to sell limited quantities into the target nation. These rents will emerge in the form of a per-unit difference between lower world prices and higher internal values inside the target nation.

SUMMARY

Export taxes and general export controls are designed and implemented by individual nations to keep domestic prices lower than international prices. The objectives of creating this kind of a price wedge are to generate tax revenue for the government, to keep internal prices for the controlled product lower than they otherwise would be, or both. With export taxes or quantitative export controls, supplies otherwise destined for export are bottled up inside the country, driving domestic prices down. If internal demand for the export-taxed item is very small or nonexistent, the levy is mainly a revenue-raising device for the government.

An export embargo is a specific suspension of sales to one or more target nations motivated by political, strategic, or military objectives that transcend commercial considerations. For a narrowly focused export embargo to be effective, stringent economic and political conditions must be met. Otherwise the embargo will weaken and fail as international transshipments and market arbitrage operations undermine the original shortage in the target nation caused by the trade suspension.

QUESTIONS

12.1 Panduras is a large banana-exporting country with almost no domestic commercial demand for bananas. The Panduran minister of the treasury argues that the highly price-inelastic supply curve for bananas inside the country means that a heavy export tax to generate government revenue will not cause a serious sacrifice in foreign exchange earnings from bananas. Is this assertion correct or not? Why?

12.2 Forestonia is a small, rather poor European country covered by densely wooded, privately owned tree farms. Much of the output of the Forestonian timber industry is suitable only for firewood, some of which traditionally has been exported to neighboring countries. Increased international demand has caused firewood production in Forestonia to exceed the nation's long-run tree replacement and reforestation programs. Formulate a program to deal with this problem by means of trade policy. Defend your program on economic grounds, keeping in mind its effects on prices (domestic and international), trade volumes, foreign exchange earnings, government revenue, etc.

12.3 Assume that following a major political disagreement the United States decides to embargo all grain exports to the nation of Kremland. Discuss the economic conditions under which such an embargo could have a long-run negative impact on Kremland's economy.

12.4 Use partial equilibrium analysis and one or more clearly labeled diagrams to illustrate how a large soybean-exporting nation could use its international market power to (1) generate export tax revenue, (2) benefit its own domestic soybean buyers, and (3) offset some or all of the social costs that arise with such a tax.

ADDITIONAL READINGS

Corden, W. M. 1971. *The Theory of Protection*, Clarendon Press, Oxford, England, pp. 15–17 and 119–121. (Short excerpts about export taxes and the symmetry of protection for exports versus imports.)

Cotterill, R. April 1980. Cartels and Embargoes as Instruments of American Foreign Policy, Agricultural Economics Report No. 373, Dept. of Agricultural Economics, Michigan State University, East Lansing, Michigan. (Basically a historical discussion of the topic and a nontechnical analysis of recent experiences written in the wake of the 1980 U.S. grain embargo against the U.S.S.R.)

Goode, R., Lent, G. E., and Ojha, P. D. November 1966. Role of export taxes in developing countries, *International Monetary Fund Staff Papers*, 13(3):453–501.

Grennes, T. 1984. *International Economics*, Prentice-Hall, Englewood Cliffs, New Jersey, pp. 177–179, 193–194, and 200–202. (Short discussions of export taxes, embargoes, and quotas in the partial equilibrium framework.)

Hillman, J. S. 1978. *Nontariff Agricultural Trade Barriers*, University of Nebraska Press, Lincoln, Nebraska, pp. 88–93. (A nontechnical discussion of export interferences generally.)

Hufbauer, G. C., and Schott, J. J. 1983. *Economic Sanctions in Support of Foreign Policy Goals*, MIT Press, Cambridge, Massachusetts. (A short book on the economics and politics of trade sanctions. Chapter 5 summarizes conditions for success of sanctions including a list of do's and don't's for policy makers.)

Schmitz, A., McCalla, A. F., Mitchell, D. O., and Carter, C. 1981. *Grain Export Cartels*, Ballinger Publishing Co., Cambridge, Massachusetts. (Chapter 4 is a mainly partial equilibrium discussion of the economics of export control.)

Part Four

Other Trade Policy Topics

I hate quotations. Tell me what you know.

Ralph Waldo Emerson

Chapter 13

Intermediate versus Final Goods: Trade and Effective Protection

In this chapter we will widen our view of agricultural production in order to consider the linkages among raw materials, intermediate goods, and final goods. The reason we need to do this is that some nations engage in international trade with both agricultural raw materials and final goods made from these raw materials. For instance, a country might import some wool, produce some wool domestically, and export woolen textiles or even wool sweaters. Another nation might produce and export feed grain yet import frozen beef.

In our previous analyses we have assumed implicitly that the domestic production of either export goods or import-competing products relies on inputs supplied totally by the domestic economy. However, agricultural production processes are often quite complex and specialized. Hence, raw materials and other intermediate goods as well as "final" products may be traded internationally. It is the economic linkage between various tradeable goods that we will examine in this chapter. In addition, we will consider some trade policy questions from this more complex perspective. This is because trade policies affecting inputs or raw materials may differ from and even conflict seriously with those affecting final goods. Similarly, protective measures on behalf of domestic input suppliers or final goods producers can have differential repercussions throughout the system that need to be illuminated.

One goal of this chapter will be to simplify an inherently complex series of ideas so that a few important economic principles can be illuminated. As mentioned, a product exported by a trading nation may contain some imported raw materials in its production. Hence, trade policy questions affecting production of this commodity can arise on both the export and the import side. Similarly, a final good imported into a nation may compete directly on the domestic market with a local product using domestic raw materials, some of which are exported and some of which may be supplemented by imports. Here, also, the trade policy intervention possibilities and interconnections are numerous even for a single trading nation. So we need a systematic but simple analytical framework around which to organize ideas about this potentially baffling topic.

ANALYTICAL FRAMEWORK

As before, our viewpoint will be that of an individual producing nation facing international markets, but now at more than one level. For clarity, we will cling to the small-nation assumption for both the final good in question and for the raw materials from which it is fashioned. More specifically, let us visualize a final product q_F that can be imported or exported. Naturally, the nation under consideration has a q_F-producing sector. Assume that the production of q_F requires a raw material q_R. The production of q_F also requires the services of a processing and handling industry, q_P.

The raw material q_R is produced domestically. It might be cotton. It can be used in the domestic production of q_F (textiles) and/or exported. However, domestic supplies of q_R can be supplemented if necessary by imports at a fixed world price. For this discussion, we adopt the view that q_P is nontradeable. That is, the services of the processing and handling sector must come fully from internal inputs. This could be a spinning, weaving, and dyeing industry. Thus we combine a tradeable but domestically produced raw material with nontradeable processing and handling services to produce a tradeable final product. Our objective with this schema is to examine the basic economics of production, trade, and possible trade policy interventions in both the q_R and q_F markets.

Next, assume that the production relationship between raw materials and processing is very simple. To produce the final product, raw materials and processing must be combined in fixed proportions, as in a recipe. This assumption, which can be relaxed in a more general analysis, allows us to use our familiar two-dimensional partial equilibrium diagrams.

Figure 13.1c is the raw material sector. The fixed world price for these raw materials is p_{WR}. Any amount of q_R can be imported or exported at p_{WR}. The domestic supply function of the raw material is SR. At domestic output less than that indicated at k, the internal supply price is less than the world price. At larger outputs, the domestic supply price is higher than the world price.

Fig. 13.1b is the domestic, nontradeable processing sector. The function SP is the domestic supply curve of q_P, processing services. The horizontal axes of Figs. 13.1c and b measure quantities of raw materials and processing ser-

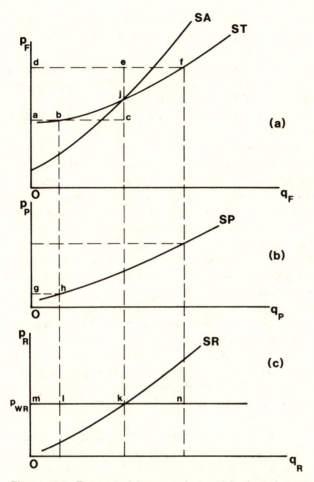

Figure 13.1 Raw material, processing, and final goods sectors

vices respectively. They are lined up with each other vertically so that each volume of q_R is uniquely associated with the specific amount of q_P directly above it. These two quantities are required to produce the vertically aligned volume of the final good q_F measured along the horizontal axis in Fig. 13.1a.

There are two final good supply curves shown in Fig. 13.1a. The first, SA, is the vertical addition of SR from Fig. 13.1c and SP from Fig. 13.1b. Hence, SA is the supply of the final good when autarky prevails in the raw material market—all raw materials and processing are obtained domestically. The function ST is the vertical addition of p_{WR} and SP. It is the supply of the final good when either foreign or domestic supplies of the raw material, obtained at p_{WR}, are combined with domestic processing services. The point in Fig. 13.1a where SA and ST cross is labeled j. It lies directly over point k of Fig. 13.1c. The vertical distance between SA and ST in Fig. 13.1a is equal to the vertical distance between SR and p_{WR}. This distance is the difference between the international and domestic supply prices of q_R at various domestic outputs of q_R.

At prices and volumes of q_F less than those associated with j, SA is below ST, reflecting the use of lower-priced domestic raw materials under autarky. At higher prices and volumes, ST lies below SA, reflecting the lower world price of the raw material relative to the domestic supply price for that volume of raw material under autarky.

Now assume that free trade prevails in the raw material sector (Fig. 13.1c). When domestic demand for the raw material is less than internal production at p_{WR} (at point k), the excess supply is exported. When domestic demand for the raw material exceeds the amount supplied at p_{WR}, the required extra volume beyond k is imported from the world market. In Fig. 13.1a, the relation of SA and ST to each other and to point j illustrates this linkage. When ST lies above and to the left of SA, domestic demand for the raw material is less than the amount produced; the excess is exported. When SA lies above and to the left of ST, the domestic raw material demand exceeds the amount supplied, and raw material imports are required.

To illustrate, consider a final goods price indicated by $0a$ in Fig. 13.1a. At that price and with free trade in q_R, the volume ab of the final good is produced. This requires the volume gh in the processing sector, supplied at a price $0g$ (Fig. 13.1b). The associated raw material needs are ml in Fig. 13.1c. The balance of domestic raw material production lk is exported at the world price of p_{WR}. In Fig. 13.1a, the segment bc indicates the volume of raw material exports expressed in terms of the final goods that could have been produced domestically.

At higher supply prices (and outputs) of the final good, more domestic raw material is used, so less is available for export. If p_F rises past point j in Fig. 13.1a, more of the final good is produced than can be manufactured with domestically supplied raw materials. Raw materials must be imported. For instance, at the supply price $0d$, the volume of q_F produced is df. At this output, the quantity of raw material imported is kn in Fig. 13.1c, with mk being supplied domestically. In Fig. 13.1a, the segment ef is the final goods equivalent of the imported raw material.

Fig. 13.2 is essentially an enlargement of Fig. 13.1a. Its purpose is to show how imports and exports of the raw material and the final product are affected by changing prices for the final good. Domestic demand for the final good is the function D, and the supply function ST is the same as in Fig. 13.1. Point j in Fig. 13.2 corresponds to point j in Fig. 13.1a. It is the point along ST at which domestic output of the final good exactly exhausts domestic raw material production. To the left of j, raw material is exported at p_{WR}; to the right, it is imported. Point a in Fig. 13.2 is the isolation equilibrium for the final good. In this specific case, point a is above and to the right of point j along ST.

With the raw material price constant at some p_{WR}, let the final goods price on the international market be either p_{F1}, p_{F2}, or p_{F3}. At p_{F1}, the final good q_F is imported in the amount *cr*. Domestic production of q_F is only *bc*. Hence, the equivalent of *cd* units of the raw material are produced but not used internally. They are exported.

At p_{F2}, smaller amounts of q_F are imported (*gh* in Fig. 13.2). However, domestic production of q_F expands to *eg* units, which more than exhausts the domestic production of the raw material. In fact, *fg* units of q_F must be produced from imported raw materials.

At p_{F3}, the nation is an exporter of q_F in the amount *ln*. To sustain the domestic q_F output at *kn*, the equivalent of *mn* units must be produced from imported raw materials. Consequently, as the world price of the final good rises, the nation in this specific situation changes from being an importer of the final good and an exporter of raw material to being an importer of both. Next, it becomes an exporter of the final good and an importer of the raw material as prices of q_F continue to rise.

Now visualize a somewhat different situation. Fig. 13.3 is similar to Fig. 13.2 except that the domestic demand curve D intersects ST at an isolation equilibrium (point *a*) below the raw material self-sufficiency point, *j*. This allows a slightly different trade and production scenario to unfold as the final good price rises from p_{F1} to p_{F2} to p_{F3}. Rather than describing the full details of Fig. 13.3, we can summarize by observing that at p_{F1} the nation imports q_F and exports q_R. As the price rises to p_{F2}, the nation becomes an exporter of q_F, yet it still exports the raw material. At p_{F3}, the expanding q_F production for export requires importation of the raw material since all domestic production of q_R is used at home.

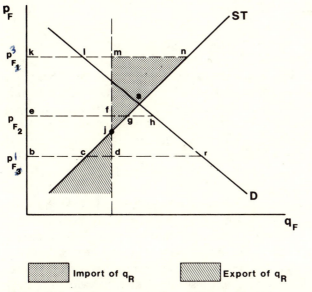

Figure 13.2 Trade and production of final goods and raw material (case 1)

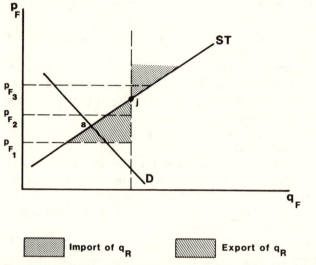

Import of q_R Export of q_R

Figure 13.3 Trade and production of final goods and raw material (case 2)

Figs. 13.1, 13.2, and 13.3 provide the fundamentals for consistent thinking about interlocked raw material and output sectors in a trading environment. Price relations can be changed, demand and supply functions can be shifted or altered in shape and, as we shall see, trade barriers can be introduced. Much of the discussion in this chapter reflects the area of reasoning and analysis that economists call the theory of "effective protection."

TRADE POLICY EFFECTS

In this section we will look at two specific illustrations of trade policy intervention to show how the interlocked raw material, processing, and final goods sectors may be affected. The first case is a fixed tariff or quota imposed on the importation of the final good. The second is a fixed tariff levied on raw material imports. These illustrations with both the raw material and the final good being imported are only two of the many that could be specified. Both can be exemplified by a nation that imports high-protein poultry feeds and frozen ready-to-cook chicken broilers.

Tariff on Final Goods

Fig. 13.4 shows some possible implications of a fixed tariff on q_F. As the tariff T is applied to q_F, imports shrink from *eb* to *cd* in Fig. 13.4*a*. Domestic production of the final good expands behind the tariff from point *e* to point *c* along *ST*. As this occurs, point *j* is passed. Recall that point *j* is the place along *ST* at which the production of q_F uses all of the domestic output of q_R. Hence, in this case, the tariff protection of q_F causes the nation to switch from exporting q_R to importing q_R.

   The movement from e to c along ST reflects a corresponding increase in the demand for nontraded processing services. Note that this output expansion bids up the price (or cost) of processing from p_{P1} to p_{P2} along SP in Fig. 13.4b. Thus, the tariff on q_F provides economic protection for processors but not for domestic producers of q_R, who still face the world price p_{WR}. (More about the extent of this intermediate good protection in a later section.) Free trade in the raw material prevents any price-changing effects of the tariff from reaching domestic producers of q_R. The response to the tariff-caused demand increase for q_R is that all domestic q_R production is used internally, then supplemented with raw material imports from the international market.

   Consider the feed grain/poultry example. This particular intervention corresponds to a new or an increased tariff being levied on imported frozen chickens. Such a move would increase domestic chicken output and expand imports of high-protein poultry feeds.

   This specific example parallels the adjustments indicated in Fig. 13.2 as the final goods price changes from p_{F1} to p_{F2}. Many other trade policy interventions in the final goods market can be investigated using this basic analytical framework—quotas, mixing regulations, export subsidies, or taxes,

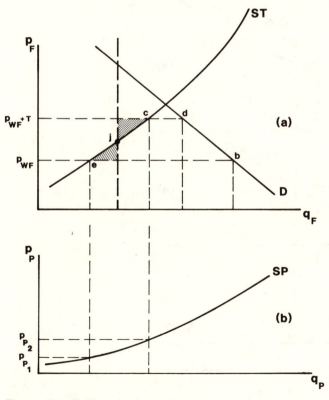

Figure 13.4 Tariff on the final good

etc. In general, if the intervention increases domestic output, the nontraded intermediate goods and services in that particular sector are protected.

If intervention decreases domestic output, the nontraded goods will sustain price and production decreases. The latter is often called "negative protection" because from the viewpoint of the nontraded sector the impacts of the policy are unfavorable.

Tariff on Raw Materials

Let us now consider the effects of a tariff on the imported raw material, with no trade policy intervention occurring in the final goods market. Fig. 13.5 reflects this case. In Fig. 13.5c, the tariff is indicated as L per imported unit of q_R. As long as domestic raw material requirements exceed the production volume indicated at point m on SR, the internal price of q_R is $p_{WR} + L$. If domestic requirements for q_R are between n and m, along SR, the supply price

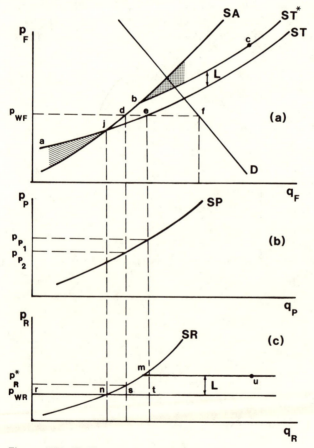

Figure 13.5   Tariff on the raw material

will be given by the domestic supply curve. In this area, the tariff L will be prohibitive for the importation of q_R. To the left of point n, the supply curve for q_R is the horizontal line at p_{WR}. This is because the raw material can be exported at its world price. Thus, the supply function for q_R, with the tariff intervention, lies along $rnmu$, where u is any point to the right of m along the horizontal line $p_{WR} + L$.

This new, tariff-laden supply curve for q_R will generate a new supply curve for q_F in Fig. 13.5a. This new function is labeled ST^*. Overall, it is indicated by $ajbc$. Up to point j from the left, ST^* is the same as ST. From j to b, ST^* lies along SA since only domestic q_R is used. Beyond b out to any point c, ST^* lies above ST by the vertical equivalent of the import levy (L) on imports of q_R. At outputs of q_F that exceed those indicated at point j, more *domestic* raw materials are used than would be the case with free trade. Consequently, beyond n, higher prices will prevail for q_R up to the maximum of $p_{WR} + L$. Raw material usage beyond point m in Fig. 13.5c (or its equivalent, point b in Fig. 13.5a) will require some q_R to be imported. These imports, as well as the domestic q_R output, will be priced internally at $p_{WR} + L$.

Now consider a specific situation in this policy context. Assume that the world price of the final good is p_{WF}. With no intervention, an amount of q_F equal to ef would be imported (Fig. 13.5a). Here, domestic production of q_F occurs at point e. At this level of domestic q_F production, Fig. 13.5c indicates that imports of q_R in the amount nt would be required, with rn being supplied by domestic producers.

The imposition of the tariff L in the raw material sector brings ST^* into play as raw material costs to domestic buyers rise. Imports of q_F increase from ef to df, causing the now more-costly domestic production of q_F to fall by de. This fall in domestic final goods output reduces activity in the processing sector (Fig. 13.5b). Prices in that sector fall from p_{P1} to p_{P2}.

Some interesting effects occur in the raw material sector (Fig. 13.5c). Since the tariff is prohibitive at point s, which is the new volume of q_R demanded, all raw material imports (nt) are snuffed out. However, domestic q_R production is protected by this tariff and expands by ns as the internal price of the raw material goes up to p_R^*. In this case, the domestic price of q_R does not increase by the full amount of the tariff. If, under other circumstances, domestic q_F output had expanded sufficiently to require raw materials beyond m, imports of q_R could resume. However, they would carry the tariff L.

This analysis would apply if our poultry-producing and importing nation placed a tariff on high-protein feed imports. To parallel the graphics just discussed, the tariff would have eliminated all feed imports for this sector. Behind this protective tariff, domestic production of feed would expand, but not enough to completely offset the fall in imports. This is because the domestic production of chicken would drop in response to higher feed prices, even though the feed-price increase was less than the per-unit value of the prohibitive tariff.

Chicken imports would expand to offset the decrease in domestic chicken output. The tariff on feed would protect the domestic feed industry but punish the chicken-producing and processing sector.

This specific illustration is only one of many that can be considered within the framework of Fig. 13.5. Some interesting manipulations of the framework can be employed to answer the questions at the end of this chapter. In general, trade policy intervention to protect raw material producers will increase the costs of, and hence the supply price of, final goods. The direct effect of such protection will be to reduce domestic output of q_F even though the internal use of locally produced q_R rises. Thus, while q_R producers are protected, the processing sector suffers from negative protection—lower output and lower prices. This will occur irrespective of whether q_F is imported or exported.

EFFECTIVE PROTECTION

The disaggregation of production stages, as visualized in this chapter, allows us to examine how a tariff or a quota on a final good, raw material, or any intermediate product may protect or damage other related sectors. Economists have called this approach the analysis of "effective protection." In principle, the effective protection idea is relatively simple, even though the complete theory and related empirical investigations may be quite complex.

In this section, we will describe some effective protection ideas within the context of Figs. 13.1 through 13.5, looking at a couple of plausible examples. In any analysis of effective protection, it is first necessary to disaggregate the value of one unit of the final product in question into its value-added components. This process may be simple or very complex. In our illustrative examples, using basic algebra, it will be simple. We will assume that the per-unit value of the final good consists of (1) the value added by the raw material and (2) the value added by the processing operations. Since we specified a very simple production relationship between q_R, q_P, and q_F, we can readily disaggregate the final value of q_F into its component parts. Using price multiplied by quantity as the relevant value measure,

$$p_F q_F = p_P(q_P) + p_R(q_R) \tag{13.1}$$

Then, dividing by q_F,

$$p_F = p_P\left(\frac{q_P}{q_F}\right) + p_R\left(\frac{q_R}{q_F}\right) \tag{13.2}$$

which can be written as

$$p_F = p_P(w_P) + p_R(w_R) \tag{13.3}$$

where w_P and w_R are the number of units of q_P and q_R needed respectively to produce one unit of q_F.

Consider a tariff on q_F, with q_R freely traded at its international price. The tariff T pushes up the domestic price of q_F to $p_F + T$. Hence, the overall or "nominal" rate of protection for q_F is r_F where

$$r_F = \frac{T}{p_F} \tag{13.4}$$

This equation expresses the relative increase in the per-unit value of q_F caused by the tariff. This increase will be captured fully by firms in the processing sector because the raw material is freely available at the world price either domestically or from foreign sellers.

Let p_P^* be the new per-unit value of q_P after the tariff on final goods is levied. Let r_P be the "effective" rate at which production of q_P is protected by T. Then

$$p_F + T = p_P^* \, w_P + p_R w_R \tag{13.5}$$

and

$$r_P = \frac{p_P^* - p_P}{p_P} \tag{13.6}$$

Simple algebra on Eqs. (13.3) and (13.5) shows that

$$p_P^* - p_P = \frac{T}{w_P} \tag{13.7}$$

and inserting Eq. (13.7) into (13.6) produces

$$r_P = \frac{T}{p_P(w_P)} \tag{13.8}$$

Note that the value added term $p_P w_P$ is always positive and, as we can see from Eq. (13.3), always smaller than p_F. Hence, r_P will always be larger than r_F. For any tariff on the final good, the rate of effective protection will be higher for the processing sector than the nominal rate of protection on the final good. In fact, the ratio of r_P to r_F will be inversely proportional to the importance of the processing sector within the total value of q_F. That is,

$$r_P > r_F \tag{13.9}$$

and

$$\frac{r_P}{r_F} = \frac{p_F(q_F)}{p_P(q_P)}$$

This line of reasoning indicates that any given nominal rate of protection for q_F will always translate into a higher rate of effective protection on q_P. This effective rate will be increasingly higher than the nominal rate the smaller the value added in the sector under consideration.

For example, suppose instant coffee is initially priced at $4.00 per jar at wholesale. Assume that the value-added component of freely imported raw coffee beans is $2.40, and the value added from the domestic processing and handling sector is $1.60. A new tariff on instant coffee of $0.80 per jar is a nominal rate of (0.80/4.00) or 20 percent. However, the effective rate of protection provided by this tariff for domestic processors is much higher—namely (0.80/1.60) or 50 percent. Note that if the processing value added had been as low as $0.80 per jar instead of $1.60, the effective rate of protection would have been 100 percent.

Next consider a tariff on the raw material, with the final good remaining freely traded. A rearrangement of the basic value-added relationship in Eq. (13.3) gives

$$p_R = p_F \left(\frac{1}{w_R}\right) - p_P \left(\frac{w_P}{w_R}\right) \tag{13.10}$$

Let the new tariff on q_R be denoted by L. Then the nominal protection rate on q_R is

$$r_R = \frac{L}{p_R} \tag{13.11}$$

where r_R is the nominal rate of protection on q_R. The tariff-laden price of q_R is now

$$p_R + L = p_F \left(\frac{1}{w_R}\right) - p_P^* \left(\frac{w_P}{w_R}\right) \tag{13.12}$$

with p_P^* being the new per-unit value of q_P after internal adjustment is made to the raw material tariff. The value of the final good does not change in this example since it is freely traded. The effective rate of protection on q_P is expressed as in Eq. (13.6).

$$r_P = \frac{p_P^* - p_P}{p_P} \tag{13.13}$$

More simple algebra on Eq. (13.3), (13.12), and (13.13) shows that

$$r_P = \frac{-L}{p_P(w_P/w_R)} \qquad (13.14)$$

Note that while the tariff on q_R makes r_R positive, it makes r_P negative. An input tariff generates negative protection for the sectors that use that input in further processing. This is because the resulting higher raw material cost puts upward pressure on the final product's domestic supply price. But because the final good in this example is freely traded, this cost increase cannot be passed along to buyers. Thus, a downward squeeze is applied to the value added in the processing sector.

This negative effective protection rate relative to the positive nominal protection on q_R is inversely proportional to the value added in processing compared with the basic raw material value. That is,

$$\frac{r_P}{r_R} = - \frac{p_R w_R}{p_P w_P} \qquad (13.15)$$

The effective protection rate for q_P will always be negative when q_R is taxed. The rate will be higher the smaller the proportion of value added in processing.

Recall the coffee example discussed earlier. Suppose that the wholesale price of the freely traded final good is $4.00 per jar, with $2.40 accounted for by imported coffee beans and $1.60 by domestic processing. Now assume that a 25 percent tariff is levied on coffee beans. The raw material costs in this case increase to $3.00 per jar. Because the wholesale price of coffee must remain at $4.00 per jar, value added in processing falls to $1.00 per jar. The nominal rate of protection for raw coffee is 25 percent, but the effective rate of protection in processing is -37.5 percent. This latter rate is both negative and higher compared with the nominal rate on coffee beans.

SUMMARY

Disaggregating any domestic production process into tradeable and nontradeable inputs (or intermediate goods) allows us to investigate the economics of trade and trade policy in both final goods and raw materials. A relatively simple demand and supply framework, carefully specified in this chapter, provides insight into the forces that lead to either imports or exports of raw materials and/or final products.

The core of this simple partial equilibrium analysis involves a final product produced from a basic raw material and the nontradeable services of a domestic processing industry. The final product may be either imported or exported from the domestic economy. The raw material is also produced domestically. In addition, this raw material may be exported if domestic production exceeds internal requirements. On the other hand, domestic raw material supplies may be supplemented by imports if domestic requirements exceed production.

This framework allows us to examine the differential impacts of tariffs or other trade policy interventions on various sectors within the trading nation. The concepts of nominal versus effective protection are especially helpful in assessing the direction and strength of these differential impacts.

QUESTIONS

13.1 Assume that the nation of Fruitland has a food processing industry that depends heavily, but not exclusively, on export sales. Fruitland itself provides the basic food commodities (fruits) and the services of a food processing industry. A major input for this industry is glass packaging materials (jars), which are partly produced domestically and partly imported.

Analyze the protective aspects of the following trade policies as they affect the food processing industry and the domestic glass industry, considering both nominal and effective protection. Also evaluate the effects of these policies on imports and exports. (Use the free market as the basis for your comparisons. Assume that Fruitland is a small part of the world markets for both fruit and glass jars.)

a A fixed export subsidy on processed food
b A fixed import subsidy on glass jars
c A fixed export tax on processed food
d A fixed import tariff on glass jars
e An import tariff on glass jars that may be refunded if the jars are exported with food products inside

13.2 The Asian country of Dyeland imports raw cotton and exports ready-to-wear clothing. Dyeland is a small part of the international cotton and textile market. However, the textile and clothing manufacturing industries provide substantial employment in the country. In addition, domestic cotton production also generates a significant amount of rural income and employment.

The Dyeland government has decided to provide a direct production subsidy to the domestic manufacturers of clothing. It is to be a specific payment from the national treasury to the numerous firms in the industry per unit of total output. Analyze and discuss the price, production, and trade consequences of this action.

ADDITIONAL READINGS

Corden, W. M. 1971. *The Theory of Protection,* Clarendon Press, Oxford, England. (The author of this book is one of the main originators of the effective protection theory; these ideas are woven throughout the volume, but see Chap. 3 especially.)

Greenaway, D. 1983. *Trade Policy and the New Protectionism,* St. Martin's Press, New York, New York, Chap. 4. (A thorough algebraic treatment of nominal versus effective protection.)

Grennes, T. 1984. *International Economics,* Prentice-Hall, Englewood Cliffs, New Jersey, pp. 206–208. (A short illustrative statement about effective protection, focusing on input tariffs versus output tariffs.)

Grubel, H. G. 1981. *International Economics,* rev. ed., Richard D. Irwin & Co., Homewood, Illinois, pp. 142–144. (Another short illustrative statement of the basic effective protection concept.)

Grubel, H. G., and Johnson, H. G. (eds.). 1971. *Effective Tariff Protection,* General Agreement on Tariffs and Trade, Graduate Institute of International Studies, Geneva, Switzerland. (Proceedings of a conference concerning numerous aspects of effective protection held during the period of the most rapid development of this theory.)

Michaely, M. 1977. *Theory of Commercial Policy,* University of Chicago Press, Chicago, Illinois, Chap. 4. (A general equilibrium treatment of this topic.)

Chapter 14

Trade Preferences

Most of the weapons in any country's trade policy arsenal are designed to promote the economic welfare of one or more groups inside the country—consumers, producers, taxpayers, and perhaps others. Virtually every topic discussed previously in this book has emphasized this tendency. However, there is one category of policy—trade preferences—that attempts to benefit designated foreign export nations at the possible expense of other foreign nations or even domestic interests. Trade preferences operate by permitting specific imported goods from specific foreign nations to enter the preference-granting nation at lower rates of duty or under more advantageous nontariff terms than are available for similar products from other nations.

THE NATURE OF TRADE PREFERENCES

Since the end of World War II, the multinational General Agreement on Tariffs and Trade (GATT) has attempted to foster widespread adherence among trading nations to the principle of "nondiscrimination" in the application of tariffs. This principle holds that within GATT importing nations must treat all foreign suppliers equally. Although there is widespread general support for this principle around the trading world, preferential trading arrangements still occur in several contexts.

Economically integrated blocs of nations, like the European Economic Community (EEC), have systematically lowered traditional trade barriers among member countries as part of the integration process. These lowered barriers are not typically available to nonmembers. This is a form of preferential trading, and it is sanctioned by GATT.

Some industrial nations, including the EEC members collectively, maintain preferential trading arrangements with numerous less-developed nations linked to these industrial nations by colonial and territorial ties from an earlier era. In addition, several developed nations have also granted trade preferences to large groups of less-developed nations for designated categories of products, including some agricultural commodities. These general preferences, also sanctioned by GATT, are not based on former political, cultural, or geographic ties. The usual criteria for inclusion in the benefited groups hinge on national income, stage of development, and political considerations.

The motives for granting trade preferences can be quite complex. On the one hand, the motivation may be relatively narrow. Nation A might grant Nation B preferential access to its canned fruit and vegetable market in return for special access to Nation B's feed grain market, neither of these concessions being available to third countries. On the other hand, the exchange of concessions might be quite broad, cutting across wide categories of goods and services. This might occur if Nations A and B are in the process of forming a free trade area, a customs union, or a common market.

In addition, the motivation for offering preferential access might be a broadly based desire by the granting government to foster economic development and growth among grantee nations through expanded trade. No matter what the motivation, the basic economic analysis of preferential trading arrangements is fundamentally the same.

We will not attempt a systematic discussion of the institutional aspects of trade preferences. However, it is important for those interested in trade policy economics to be acquainted with some of the terms encountered in discussions of trade preferences, especially those relating to the trade aspects of economic integration.

Economic Integration   The drawing together of nations such that the movement of goods and services (and maybe factors of production) is freer between the members themselves than between members and nonmembers. Some integration of economic, financial, and social policies and institutions may occur in advanced stages of integration. The main categories of economic integration are free trade areas, customs unions, common markets, and economic federations.

Free-Trade Area   The members of a free-trade area lower or eliminate tariffs and perhaps other trade barriers among themselves on broad categories of products, but each maintains its own independent trade policy toward nonmember nations. No other economic integration among members occurs.

Customs Union   A customs union involves the internal lowering or elimination of trade barriers as with a free-trade area *plus* the establishment of a common trade policy toward nonmembers. No deliberate integration of factor markets or other economic policy occurs.

Common Market   A common market is basically a customs union *plus* some integration of markets for factors of production such as labor, capital, and enterprise. Some partial alignment of tax, fiscal, agricultural, and monetary policy may occur in a common market. Consequently, the delegation of some limited economic decision-making powers to a supranational authority also may be involved.

Economic Federation (or Union)   An economic federation pushes integration substantially beyond that of a common market. Factor markets as well as product markets are closely integrated. Substantial unification occurs in fiscal, monetary, taxation, and social policies. The original national demarcations between the members become increasingly blurred. Full political integration vis-à-vis the rest of the world denotes an advanced stage of economic federation.

THE ANALYTICAL SETTING

In this section we examine the partial equilibrium economics of trade preferences from the viewpoint of the importing nation that grants them. It really does not matter for this argument whether the preferences arise from the implementation of a system of general preferences or from the formation of an integrated economic unit like a customs union.

To discuss trade preferences, we propose a simple but relatively general setting. Let us assume that our point of view is that of Nation A, an importer of the product in question, say, sugar. Nation B is another country that produces sugar. However, Nation B's costs of producing sugar are high enough so that it cannot compete as a sugar exporter on a free trade basis with exporters from the rest of the world.

Initially, Nation A protects its own domestic sugar growers with a fixed tariff applied in a nondiscriminatory way against all sugar from all exporters. In this initial situation, Nation A imports sugar from numerous sellers at a constant world price, but none from Nation B. Now suppose that Nation A grants Nation B preferential access to its sugar market. In particular, imagine that sugar from Nation B now enjoys duty-free access into A, but everyone else's sugar is still subject to the original tariff. Let us examine the production, price, and trade implications of this policy change.

ANALYSIS OF PREFERENCES

The basics of the original situation are reflected in Fig. 14.1. The domestic demand and supply relationships for Nation A are shown in Fig. 14.1a. The

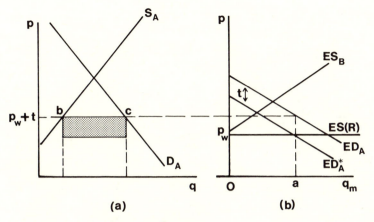

Figure 14.1 Trade without preferences

excess demand curves for Nation A with and without the tariff (t) are shown in Fig. 14.1b as ED^* and ED respectively. The excess supply curve of the rest of the world, excluding Nation B, is shown as $ES(R)$. The excess sugar supply of Nation B is shown as ES_B. The notion that B is a relatively high-cost sugar producer is reflected in the diagram. For any volume of sugar exports, Nation B's supply price is higher than $ES(R)$, which forms the world price. Thus the world price of sugar is p_W and, in the original situation, B exports no sugar.

Nation A imports a volume of sugar equal to $0a$ at p_W and levies the tariff (t). The domestic price of sugar is then $p_W + t$ in Fig. 14.1a. Domestic growers produce at point b along S_A, domestic buyers consume at point c along D_A. Sugar imports are equivalent to bc in Fig. 14.1a. Tariff revenue generated by Nation A's government is shown as the shaded area in Fig. 14.1a. No sugar is purchased from B since its supply price plus the tariff is always higher than $p_W + t$.

Now consider preferential access of B's sugar into Nation A—no tariff is levied on it. Figure 14.2 shows this situation. This figure is basically the same as Fig. 14.1a. However, with no tariff to face, Nation B's sugar exports compete directly with A's domestic sugar industry. The total tariff-free supply of sugar in Nation A is shown as S_{A+B}. This function is the horizontal sum of S_A and ES_B from Fig. 14.1. (Incidentally, the horizontal difference between S_{A+B} and S_A is ES_B.)

Sugar from the rest of the world can still enter Nation A at $p_W + t$ as before, so the sugar price inside A cannot rise above $p_W + t$. Because sugar producers from A and B together cannot fill A's total sugar demand at $p_W + t$, some additional, tariff-laden imports will still be required. In fact, an amount equal to eb will be produced by A's growers, bd will be imported (tariff-free) from B, and dc will be required from the rest of the world.

Total shipments of sugar into A in this illustration will not change. However, Nation B will supply sugar formerly provided by outsiders. This occurs even though Nation B is a higher-cost sugar producer than the outside

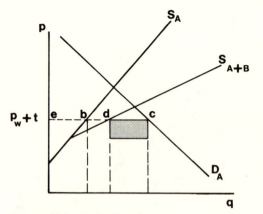

Figure 14.2 Trade diversion

exporters. This switch in trade volume from a low-cost supplier to a higher-cost supplier is called *trade diversion*. In this case, the trade volume *bd* is diverted from other suppliers to Nation B as a consequence of the preferential agreement and the resulting protection for B's sugar industry. Note also that Nation A's government relinquishes the tariff revenue that otherwise would have been collected on the import volume *bd*. The now-decreased tariff revenue is shown as the shaded area in Fig. 14.2.

Now imagine that Nation B becomes a more efficient, lower-cost sugar producer than before. Its supply price for various export volumes could be expected to fall. The total supply function, S_{A+B} in Fig. 14.2, would move to the right, approaching point *c* from above. If this occurs, it is clear that sugar shipments from B into A would increase as more and more export trade is diverted from the rest of the world to Nation B. When S_{A+B} finally intersects D_A at point *c*, trade diversion will be complete. Nation B will be the sole international sugar supplier to A at the internal price of $p_W + t$. Nation A's domestic growers will continue to produce *eb* units of sugar.

Imagine that as sugar productivity in B increases, S_{A+B} moves sufficiently far to the right so that a situation like that in Fig. 14.3 emerges. In this case, D_A, S_A, and $p_W + t$ are the same as before. However, S_{A+B} is positioned far enough to the right so that at an internal price of $p_W + t$, sugar growers in A and B together would produce more than the total amount demanded at point *c*.

In this instance, sugar prices inside A would fall to p_1 where S_{A+B} intersects D_A at point *f*. Because p_1 is lower than $p_W + t$, the trade diversion to B from the rest of the world is complete. But other adjustments also occur as a result of this domestic price decrease inside A. Total sugar imports into A from B expand from *bc* to *mf* as the quantity demanded increases and as domestic production in A falls in response to lower prices. Even though Nation B is still a relatively high-cost sugar producer compared with the rest of the world, it is efficient enough to displace some of the higher-cost sugar production in Nation A.

Comparing the two situations in Fig. 14.3, with and without the preferences, we can say that the preferential policy in Nation B's favor induced trade diversion equal to *bc*. In addition, new trade equal to *gh* plus *jk* occurred. This new trade volume is called *"trade creation,"* since it was a result of the preferential policy and did not exist previously. In general, trade creation occurs (1) when higher-cost domestic products are displaced by relatively lower-cost foreign commodities (*gh*), and/or (2) when lower internal prices induce an expansion in total consumption (*jk*) that is met by imports. Although not shown in Fig. 14.3, all tariff revenues or quota rents that might have accrued in the original situation are wiped out when the trade diversion to Nation B is complete.

WELFARE ASPECTS

We will not undertake a thorough evaluation of the economic welfare implications of trade preferences. However, we can identify some general results that occur within the preference-granting nation.

A trade preference scheme that only results in trade diversion but no domestic price reduction displays relatively modest welfare effects. If internal prices do not change, there are no adjustments in consumer or producer surplus. However, the tariff revenue formerly collected on dutiable imports now diverted to the preferred seller is lost. It becomes part of the economic value gained by the preferred seller as a result of the scheme.

If the preference scheme results in a lowering of internal prices, trade creation occurs along with trade diversion. More complex welfare adjustments

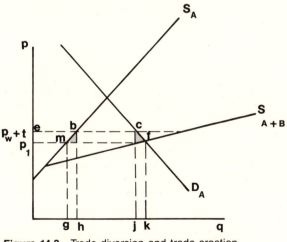

Figure 14.3 Trade diversion and trade creation

emerge. These adjustments are parallel to those that would occur if a tariff is lowered or an import quota expanded. The price decrease from $p_w + t$ to p_1 in Fig. 14.3 increases consumer surplus, reduces producer surplus, and redistributes part of the previously collected tariff value from the government to consumers. This is basically the reverse of the effects of a tariff increase, discussed in Chap. 5.

The two shaded triangular areas in Fig. 14.3 indicate the net social gains achieved by the granting nation. The shaded area under the supply curve measures the technical efficiency gain for the economy as variable resources no longer used for protected production move to other uses in the society. The shaded area under the demand curve measures the gain in consumer surplus associated with the increase in consumption occasioned by the fall in price. Finally, the balance of the previous tariff revenue, the per-unit value of which is $p_1 - p_w$, is redistributed to the preferred exporter on the total amount of trade diversion.

SUMMARY

Trade preferences are granted by importing nations to favor exports from specifically designated foreign countries. Shipments from the preferred exporters into the preference-granting importer enter under more advantageous terms than are available for similar products from elsewhere. Preferences may be granted for a variety of reasons, including the desire by the grantor to foster economic development in the favored exporter. The formation of integrated economic blocs such as customs unions and common markets requires that members systematically and preferentially reduce trade barriers among themselves relative to those confronting nonmembers. The establishment of trade preferences, for whatever reason, may result in trade diversion, trade creation, or both, depending on the nature of the preferential agreement and the supply characteristics of the trading nations involved.

QUESTIONS

14.1 Is it possible for a trade preference scheme to result in trade creation but not trade diversion? If so, illustrate this pure trade creation scheme. If not, explain why not.

14.2 The banana-exporting country of Panduras has traditionally levied a fixed export tax on its banana shipments to all importing nations. However, as a result of its entry into a newly formed customs union with several neighboring countries, Panduras lowers its export tax rate to member importers but not to outsiders. Discuss the economic effects of this development on the Panduran economy. Can you identify the exporter equivalent of trade diversion and trade creation effects?

14.3 As part of the customs union agreement mentioned in question 2, Panduras entirely eliminates its previous import tariffs on wheat from member exporters.

Moreover, the overall agreement also requires Panduras to lower, but not eliminate, its import tariff on nonmembers' wheat. Illustrate and discuss the economic effects of this aspect of the agreement, including potential trade creation and trade diversion.

14.4 Recall the arguments illustrated by Figs. 14.1, 14.2, and 14.3. How would your discussion and analysis of these matters change if the protective measures in question were import quotas rather than tariffs?

ADDITIONAL READINGS

Balassa, B. 1961. *The Theory of Economic Integration*, Richard D. Irwin, Homewood, Illinois. (The classic text on economic integration.)

Caves, R. E. and Jones, R. W. 1981. *World Trade and Payments: An Introduction*, 3rd ed., Little, Brown and Co., Boston, Massachusetts, Chap. 14. (Partial equilibrium approach to trade creation, diversion, and preferences.)

Grennes, T. 1984. *International Economics*, Prentice-Hall, Englewood Cliffs, New Jersey, pp. 202–214. (Partial equilibrium economics of trade creation, diversion, and preferences.)

Machlup, F. 1977. *A History of Thought on Economic Integration*, Columbia University Press, New York, New York. (An extensive review of economic thought on integration and trade.)

Robson, P. (ed.) 1972. *International Economic Integration*, Penguin Books, Middlesex, England. (A collection of well-known economic papers in this area.)

Sorenson, V. L. 1975. *International Trade Policy: Agriculture and Development*, Michigan State University, International and Business Studies, East Lansing, Michigan, pp. 199–208. (A nontechnical discussion of generalized preferences and economic integration as they affect agricultural trade.)

Chapter 15

Currency Exchange Rates and Trade Policy

Throughout the 1970s and early 1980s, major changes occurred in the entire international financial network. Part of this change was a major increase in the day-to-day and week-to-week volatility of currency exchange rates among most trading nations. This phenomenon reflected a broad-based move toward more flexibility in the pricing of one nation's currency in relation to other national monies. Flexible and changing exchange rates have important implications for trade policy decisions in agriculture and elsewhere. Exchange rate movements can easily swamp or obscure the desired price, trade, and production effects of any specific agricultural commodity policy. Because of the pervasive impact of exchange rate adjustments on total trade flows and values, it is important that students of agricultural trade policies have at least a rudimentary knowledge of how currency exchange rates affect commodity markets and prices.

Exchange rates among national currencies are simply the prices of one nation's money in terms of other currencies. At any specific moment, they represent the terms by which domestic prices, costs, and other values for goods and services are translated from the domestic economy onto the broader, international scene. Exchange rate adjustments typically influence national economic activity by affecting a broad array of industries, products, and occupations. Consequently, individual commodity or sectoral interests can be dominated by aggregate economic forces and policy. Hence, in a flexible regime, traditional trade policy decisions can be made with less freedom of action and much less certainty of result than if exchange rates were fixed.

In this chapter we will not attempt to describe or analyze either the complex economics of exchange rate determination or the underlying processes of adjustment through time. That would carry us far into the realm of macroeconomics and general equilibrium trade theory. Our more modest goal in this chapter is (1) to establish some basic ideas about currency exchange rates as a set of interrelated prices, (2) to use these ideas to probe the partial equilibrium economics of how exchange rate changes affect international commodity markets and prices, and (3) to discuss such topics as overvaluation, undervaluation, and multiple exchange rates.

Our approach here will be to assume that the flow of causality and reaction is from externally determined exchange rates to international agricultural product markets. We will not consider the feedback or economywide aspects here. Hence, our discussion will not involve international balance of payments issues, the dynamics of exchange rate adjustments, forward markets for traded currencies, or exchange rates and inflation. These are important topics, but beyond the scope of this book. Exchange rate policy is clearly macroeconomic trade policy. Except for some aspects of multiple exchange rate schemes, to be discussed later, it does not fit easily into the typical analytical approach employed thus far.

Even with our relatively narrow focus, it is still true that clear thinking about exchange rates is not easy. To cope with this inherent complexity, we adopt a rather simplified framework—a three-nation trading world in which both importing and exporting nations are represented in partial equilibrium style.

SOME BASIC IDEAS

Think of three trading nations, A, B, and C, with separate national currencies called alphas (α), betas (β), and gammas (γ) respectively. Imagine also that these three national currencies can be freely traded for each other on international money markets. Thus, we can visualize each of these currencies as a commodity that at any time has a known market price in terms of each of the other two.

For each alpha, there is a beta price and a gamma price. For instance, the beta price of an alpha (which we might write as β/α) is the number of betas you can obtain by selling one alpha. There is an alpha and a gamma price for each beta, and an alpha and a beta price for each gamma. These add up to six possible currency prices. But three of these exchange rates are merely reciprocals of the other three. That is, if you can get two betas for one alpha ($\beta/\alpha = 2$), in a simple and open currency market you can get 0.5 alphas by selling one beta ($\alpha/\beta = 1/2 = 0.5$).

Even after the three reciprocals are set aside, the three remaining currency prices reflect only *two* fully independent exchange rates. An open functioning currency market will ensure that once two of the three remaining exchange rates are established, the third is also determined. To illustrate this idea, imagine that we are citizens of country A, equipped with some α's. We face two international exchange rates directly—namely, the number of β's we can obtain per α (β/α) and the number of γ's we can obtain per α (γ/α). (The number of our α's that other people can obtain for their β's and γ's are the respective reciprocals, α/β and α/γ.)

Suppose the two market-determined exchange rates that we, as α holders, face are the following:

$$\frac{\beta}{\alpha} = 0.8 \tag{15.1}$$

$$\frac{\gamma}{\alpha} = 1.2 \tag{15.2}$$

Aside from the reciprocals of Eqs. (15.1) and (15.2), the only other exchange rate of interest in this three-country situation is the number of β's that can be obtained for each γ (β/γ). However, the equilibrium β/γ exchange rate is already implied as the ratio of Eq. (15.1) to Eq. (15.2). That is,

$$\frac{\beta}{\gamma} = \frac{\beta}{\alpha} \div \frac{\gamma}{\alpha} \tag{15.3}$$

$$= 0.8 \div 1.2$$

$$= 0.67$$

So, 0.67 β's can be obtained per γ; reciprocally, 1.5 γ's can be obtained per β.

Thinking beyond our three-country setting, we can show that with four trading nations there will be three independent exchange rates, with five trading nations there will be four independent exchange rates, and so on. In general, with n trading nations there will be $n - 1$ independent exchange rates.

If our currency (α) falls in value, we can obtain fewer β's and/or γ's than before. We can say that the α has *depreciated* or has experienced *devaluation*. On the other hand, if our α's increase in value so that we can obtain more β's and/or γ's than before, we say that the α has *appreciated* or has experienced *revaluation*. If the α depreciates relative to the β, this implies, conversely, that the β has appreciated in value relative to the α. Being able to get fewer β's when you sell one α naturally means you can get more α's when you sell one β.

If our α appreciates relative to the β but depreciates relative to the γ, the value of γ's must appreciate in the market relative to β's. Otherwise, currency dealers could make huge profits by arbitraging in the markets for the three currencies—selling more valuable α's for β's, for instance, trading them for γ's at the old γ/β rate, and finally exchanging those γ's for more α's than they originally started with. In fact, as α's appreciate relative to β's, the behavior of currency holders and traders will turn in this direction and the resulting market pressures will pull up the market value of γ's relative to β's. This example and others like it indicate that across the trading world, currency exchange rates are interlocked but also capable of independent adjustment.

ANALYTICAL SETTING

In all our previous analyses, we have implicitly assumed that one currency could be exchanged for another at a fixed and unchanging rate. Hence, the question of what currency to use to measure prices and values across international borders was was not really important for our theoretical inquiry. Now let us abandon that view. Let us investigate how shifting currency exchange rates affect our partial equilibrium analysis in international commodity markets.

For the moment, visualize the α as the currency on which we will focus our attention. This might be because (1) we are especially interested in the economics of Nation A's trade, (2) because the α is a major currency in which international assets are held, or (3) because the α is the currency in which world prices are usually quoted for products of interest. For the rest of this chapter, let Nation B always be a net importer of q (the product in question) and let Nation C always be a net exporter of q. This situation is shown in the lower panels of Fig. 15.1. The excess demand for q by Nation B is priced in β's and is labeled ED_B. The excess supply of q by Nation C is shown as ES_C priced in terms of γ's.

In the upper panels of Fig. 15.1, the excess demand and supply curves of Nation B and C *are priced in α's*, with the horizontal axes remaining the same. At the initial exchange rates of α's for β's and α's for γ's (say, $1\,\alpha = 1\,\beta = 1\,\gamma$), ED_B is the same as ED_B^0 and ES_C is the same as ES_C^0. In this diagram and those that follow, the superscript notation on excess demand and supply curves will indicate that the original national curve has been expressed in terms of another currency—namely, α's. Hence, ED_B^0 indicates that the excess demand of Nation B, measured originally in β's, is now expressed in terms of α's at some given exchange rate between α's and β's. Similarly, ES_C^0 is the α-priced equivalent of Nation's C's ES_C curve at a given α to γ exchange rate.

To help illustrate these ideas, pick any point a and any point g on the horizontal axes of Nations B and C respectively. The vertical line segment ab is equal to segment ce for Nation B. For Nation C, gh is equal to jl. This equality indicates that $1\,\alpha = 1\,\beta = 1\,\gamma$ in the original situation. These line segments are identified simply to help show how the relative positions of the ED and ES curves change as exchange rates alter.

First, let the β and the γ appreciate relative to the α. This is the same

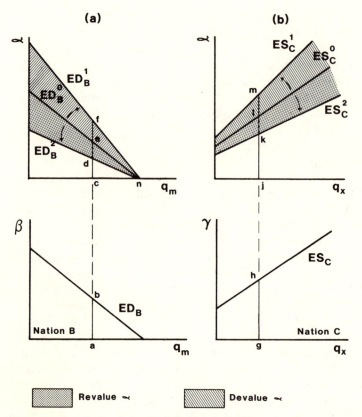

Figure 15.1   Effects of devaluation and revaluation

as a general devaluation of α. Each β will command more α's than before, so the translation of ED_B from β's into α's will generate an excess demand function like ED_B^1. At an import quantity point like a, the "new" excess demand curve measured in α's will pass through point f rather than point e. The ratio ef to ce is a measure of the extent of β's appreciation. An exactly comparable argument generates ES_C^1 on the Nation C side of Fig. 15.1, with the ratio lm to jl measuring the extent of γ's appreciation relative to α. Therefore, devaluation of the currency of interest α rotates B's demand for imports outward to the right around point n when it is measured in that particular currency. Conversely, devaluation of α rotates C's supply of exports upward and to the left in terms of that devalued currency. The more α is devalued relative to β and γ, the more ED_B^1 and ES_C^1 will rotate away from ED_B^0 and ES_C^0 respectively.

Now if β's and γ's are devalued relative to the α, exactly the reverse argument produces ED_B^2 and ES_C^2 in Fig. 15.1. Here the α is revalued relative to both other currencies. The appreciation of α compared with β and γ causes the excess demand curve, denominated in α's, to rotate downward and to the left to ED_B^2. The corresponding excess supply curve rotates downward and to the right to ES_C^2. The ratios of *ed* to *ce* and *lk* to *jl* indicate the extent of the devaluation of β and γ respectively. The stronger the appreciation of α, the more ED_B^2 and ES_C^2 rotate.

Because currency exchange-rate changes are proportional alterations in per-unit values, the negatively sloped excess demand curve will seem to pivot on its *q*-axis intercept (point *n* in Fig. 15.1), turning clockwise for a devaluation of the currency on the vertical axis and counterclockwise for an appreciation of that currency. The positively sloped excess supply curve also seems to pivot on its quantity-axis intercept (not visible in Fig. 15.1), turning counterclockwise for a devaluation of the currency on its vertical axis and clockwise for an appreciation of that currency.

From the point of view of a particular country (say A) and its national currency (say α), devaluation rotates excess demand curves displayed by foreign nations outward (to the right) and excess supply curves displayed by foreign nations backward (to the left). Appreciation (or revaluation) has the reverse effect, rotating foreign excess demand curves to the left and foreign excess supply curves to the right.

To see how exchange-rate adjustments affect trade and prices, we need to bring excess demand and supply functions together, then alter currency values. To do this in a relatively simple way, we will again adopt the viewpoint of Nation A, considering the α as either "our" currency or the main international medium of exchange. We also will retain the notion that Nation B is a net importer of the product *q* and that Nation C is a net exporter.

If Nation A is an exporter of *q*, Nation B is our international customer and Nation C is our international competitor. If Nation A is a net importer of *q*, Nation C is our supply source, also sought by Nation B for its own import requirements. To make the following arguments more realistic, we can easily consider that the excess demand curve labeled with a B is a composite of numerous foreign importing countries and that the excess supply curve labeled with a C is a similar composite of foreign exporters—foreign, that is, from Nation A's viewpoint.

Figure 15.2 expands on the format of Fig. 15.1. It is the same as Fig. 15.1 in the panels for Nations B and C (on the right). The panel for Nation A depicts A as a net exporter of *q*. The excess supply of Nation A, denominated in α's, is labeled ES_A. The function *ED(R)* is the excess demand for the rest of the world. It is the horizontal difference between ED_B^0 and ES_C^0 at various α prices. In Fig. 15.2, with fixed exchange rates among α, β, and γ, the dotted lines represent the equilibrium prices in the various currencies, the amount exported by A, the amount imported by B, and the other exports supplied by C.

One could easily draw a counterpart diagram to Fig. 15.2 in which Nation A, viewed as a net importer, would display an excess demand function to interact with a rest-of-world excess supply function, formed as the horizontal difference between ES_C^0 and ES_B^0.

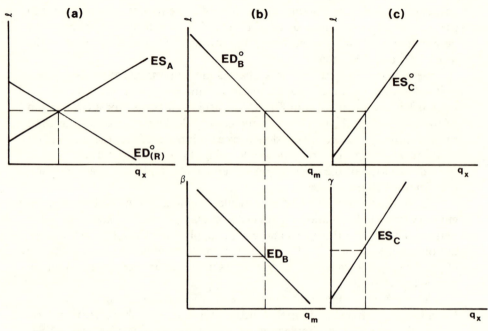

Figure 15.2   Three-nation trade equilibrium at fixed exchange rates

TRADE EFFECTS OF EXCHANGE RATE CHANGES

With three nations in our purview, there are six fundamental exchange-rate scenarios to consider. Three involve A as an importer and three involve A as an exporter. Each includes devaluation and revaluation of α, β, and γ relative to the other two currencies. The following list describes the central characteristics of each of these six scenarios from the viewpoint of Nation A—the first three with A as an exporter and the next three with A as an importer.

Nation A as an Exporter of q

1 The α is devalued or revalued relative to both the β and γ. The economics of this scenario indicates how an exporter's situation alters as its currency changes in value relative to the currencies of both its importing customers and its competing exporters.

2 The β is devalued or revalued relative to both the α and γ. The economics of this scenario indicates how an exporter's situation alters as the currency value of a major importer changes relative to all exporters.

3 The γ is devalued or revalued relative to both the α and β. This scenario illustrates how an exporter's position alters as the currency of one or more of its competing exporters changes relative to the rest of the world, including importers.

Nation A as an Importer of q

4 The α is devalued or revalued relative to both the β and γ. The economics of this scenario indicates how an importer's situation alters as its currency changes in value relative to the currencies of its supply sources and other importers of the same product.

5 The β is devalued or revalued relative to both the α and γ. This scenario illustrates how an importer's situation alters when a competing importer's currency changes relative to its own currency and to those of all exporters.

6 The γ is devalued or revalued relative to both the α and β. The economics of this scenario shows how an importer's situation changes as the exporter's currency changes relative to *all* importers.

For our purpose in this chapter, it is not necessary to provide a complete analytical discussion of all six of these exchange-rate scenarios. With the ideas that emerge in discussing three of them, the reader can construct a general system for examining the other three, plus additional complications as desired. The three scenarios to be discussed here in some detail are scenarios 1 and 2 with A as an exporter and scenario 4 with A as an importer.

Alpha Value Changes: A as Exporter (Scenario 1)

Imagine that the α is either devalued or revalued relative to both the β and γ—no change occurs in the relative value of the β vis-à-vis the γ. The partial equilibrium economics of this situation is shown in Fig. 15.3. These changes appear as clockwise and counterclockwise rotations of the excess demand and supply functions denominated in α's. The original position before any exchange-rate changes occur is indicated by the system of dotted lines in Fig. 15.3. Hence, the effects of devaluation or appreciation are reflected as movements away from this pattern of prices, production, and trade.

Consider first a devaluation of the α. The α will now be exchanged for fewer units of the importer's β and fewer units of the competing exporter's γ than before. In Fig. 15.3, this change is indicated by the clockwise rotation in B's excess demand curve from ED_B^0 to ED_B^1 and in the counterclockwise rotation of C's excess supply curve from ES_C^0 to ES_C^1. Together, this increase in demand and decrease in competitive supply (expressed in α's) generates an increase in the total excess demand function faced by A as an exporter—from $ED^0(R)$ to $ED^1(R)$. With no other changes occurring in the system, Nation A responds by increasing its exports, as reflected in the left-most panel of Fig. 15.3.

Because the net international excess demand facing Nation A increases (rotates toward the right), the α price of q increases as indicated. Although the α price of q increases, the α devaluation process reflected in ED_B^1 and ES_C^1 causes both the β and γ prices to fall, as shown in the lower panels of Fig. 15.3. As a consequence, more is imported by Nation B and less is exported by Nation C. Nation A's export market share will increase as its total imports

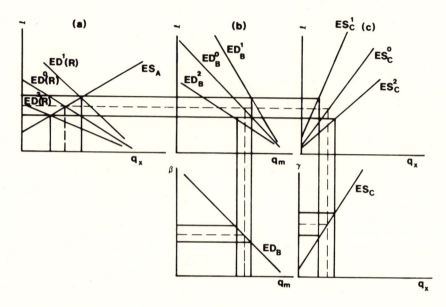

Figure 15.3 Change in α with A as exporter

increase and as competitive exports fall. The price effects of an α devaluation are split between a rise in the α price and a fall in prices expressed in other currencies.

A revaluation or appreciation of the α has exactly opposite effects. These are illustrated in Fig. 15.3 as a consequence of ED_B^0 rotating to ED_B^2 and ES_C^0 rotating to ES_C^2. Since these changes indicate a decrease in demand by B and an increase in the competitive supply from C, the net excess demand facing Nation A rotates to the left—from $ED^0(R)$ to $ED^2(R)$. With nothing else occurring, Nation A responds by decreasing its exports along ES_A as it is pushed out of shrinking international markets by the competitive exporter C.

This rearrangement in total trade and market share occurs because prices expressed in α's fall, while prices expressed in β's and γ's rise as ED_B^2 and ES_C^2 become relevant. The β price rise puts downward pressure on total imports, but the γ price rise generates export expansion by C. Together, these movements squeeze Nation A into a smaller trade volume at a lower α price. Thus, the price effects of a revaluation in α are split between a fall in the α price and an increase in the β and γ prices of the product in question.

All Exporters' Currency Values Change: A as Exporter (Scenario 2)

In this scenario, the currency values of both exporter nations, A and C, move together relative to that of the importer, B. For simplicity, we will consider only the situation in which both the α and the γ change relative to the β, but not relative to each other. The partial equilibrium economics of this scenario is shown in Fig. 15.4. The layout and interpretation of this figure parallel those of Fig. 15.3, the original position being indicated by the network of dotted lines.

In this case, joint devaluation or appreciation of the α and γ relative to the β are depicted as rotation in the excess demand function of Nation B, expressed with α's on the vertical axis. Devaluation of the exporters' currencies results in the rightward rotation from ED_B^0 to ED_B^1 in the B panel and, consequently, in the rightward rotation from $ED^0(R)$ to $ED^1(R)$ in the A panel. Note that ES_C^0 does not change position. This is because there is no change in the value of α relative to γ. This adjustment generates an increase in the α and γ prices of q, to which both A and C respond by increasing exports.

The increase in total exports is accommodated by an expansion in the quantity of imports purchased by B as a consequence of the falling β price. Both exporters share in this expansion. How much of the increase goes to each exporter is determined by the relative price responsiveness (or elasticity) of ES_A compared with that of ES_C^0. When more than one exporter devalues relative to importers, the potential trade increase for any devaluing seller is less than if it were the only one to devalue.

The reverse argument for a revaluation in α and γ relative to β is also summarized in Fig. 15.4, with the rotation of EB_B^0 to ED_B^2 and of $ED^0(R)$ to $ED^2(R)$. Markets for revaluing exporters shrink as the price effects are split

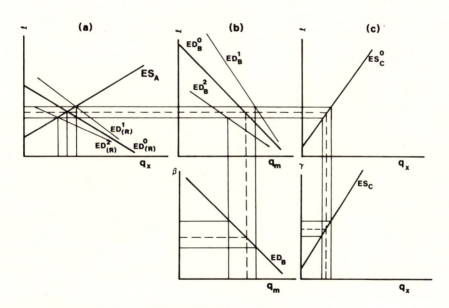

Figure 15.4 Exporters' currencies change relative to importers'

between a fall in the α and γ prices and an increase in the β price, the latter forcing a contraction in total imports of the product in question.

Alpha Value Changes: A as Importer (Scenario 3)

This scenario is similar in some ways to the first one—α changing in value relative to the β and γ. However, in this instance, we change our viewpoint to consider Nation A as an importer of q rather than an exporter. This switch in trading status for Nation A does not change the basic diagrammatics for Nations B and C. But it does cause us to reverse the sense of the excess demand and supply curves depicted for Nation A. In Fig. 15.5, the demand function ED_A in the A panel is the excess demand for imports registered by Nation A at various α prices. The import supply function facing buyers in Nation A is $ES^0(R)$ at the original exchange rate. This function is the horizontal difference between the excess supply of total exports ES_C^0 and the excess demand of other importers, ED_B^0. Again, the original position is denoted by dotted lines.

First, assume that α is devalued relative to both β and γ. In this case, ED_B^0 rotates to ED_B^1 and ES_C^0 rotates to ES_C^1. Together, these shifts imply a movement of $ES^0(R)$ to $ES^1(R)$. The lowered purchasing power of the α in international markets produces upward pressure on α prices and, consequently, a decrease in the amount of imports demanded by Nation A.

This decrease in imports into A means that the additional availability of

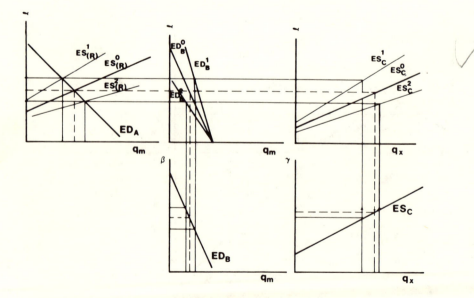

Figure 15.5 Change in α with A as importer

export supplies on the world market will press down prices expressed in β's and γ's. More will be imported by B at lower β prices, but less total exports will be supplied by C at decreased γ prices (Fig. 15.5). So the shrinkage in purchases by the devaluing importer (A) is accounted for by larger imports elsewhere and by smaller total supplies on the world market. As usual, the price effects are split between the devaluing nation, whose domestic prices increase, and the others, whose domestic prices decrease.

Revaluation of α when A is an importer produces opposite price, trade, and market share effects than those just discussed for α devaluation (Fig. 15.5). Prices in the revalued currency fall, while prices in terms of the other currencies rise. More is imported by the revaluing nation A than previously. These additional imports are drawn both from increased exports from international suppliers and decreased takings by other importers. These effects occur as ES_C^0 rotates to ES_C^2 and ED_B^0 rotates to ED_B^2. Together, they cause $ES^0(R)$ to shift to $ES^2(R)$.

OVERVALUED AND UNDERVALUED EXCHANGE RATES

Economic theory and common sense both suggest that with freely operating markets for national currencies, equilibrium or balanced exchange rates would tend to emerge. Because currency exchange rates are fundamentally prices, equilibrium rates would continually reflect the net effect of all economic, political, and social forces at play on international transactions. Exchange rates would certainly change from period to period, but these changes would not reflect deliberate intervention by national governments to change the relative value of their own or other currencies.

When governments intervene in exchange-rate determination, domestic currency values relative to foreign currencies can be pushed or set either higher or lower than they would otherwise be. They can be "overvalued" or "undervalued" respectively. Overvaluation and undervaluation are, in reality, subjective ideas since equilibrium exchange rates generally are unknown.

Government intervention in exchange-rate determination can be direct or indirect. Direct intervention occurs (1) when a national government sets its currency exchange rates officially, then controls domestic access to foreign currency and foreign access to domestic currency through administrative mechanisms, or (2) when the government buys or sells domestic and foreign currencies in sufficient amounts to hold the international price of domestic currency at either some specific value or within some relatively narrow band relative to other monies. Indirect intervention, on the other hand, occurs when sustained government activity affecting the money supply, inflation, interest rates, or other factors leads to an overvaluation or undervaluation of the nation's exchange rate as a side effect.

Whether or not any particular exchange-rate overvaluation or undervaluation is caused by direct or indirect intervention and why such action is taken are beyond the scope of this book. In the following sections we will examine the price, trade, and production effects in commodity markets of both an overvalued and an undervalued currency.

Overvaluation

Suppose that a national government overvalues its currency. Imagine, for instance, that Nation A systematically sells its holdings of β's and γ's on foreign exchange markets in order to buy α's. As long as Nation A is able to sell β's and γ's, the α will be "overvalued" since its price will be higher than it would be otherwise. Suppose the original exchange-rate pattern was $1\,\alpha = 1\,\beta = 1\,\gamma$. Purchases of α's by Nation A's government would pull up the exchange value of α to perhaps $1\,\alpha = 1.4\,\beta = 1.4\,\gamma$.

The effect of this overvaluation in international markets involving Nation A is similar to the revaluation effects depicted as the relevant functions shift from $ED^0(R)$ to $ED^2(R)$ in Fig. 15.3 and from $ES^0(R)$ to $ES^2(R)$ in Fig. 15.5. From the exporter's point of view (Fig. 15.3), overvaluation causes a foreign demand shrinkage, resulting in a decrease of export volume and prices. It is like an export tax levied by A on itself. From the importer's viewpoint (Fig. 15.5), overvaluation causes an outward shift in the foreign supply function, resulting in an increase of imports and a fall in domestic prices. It is like an import subsidy applied by A's government.

By curtailing exports and stimulating imports, overvaluation of a currency presses down domestic prices, tends to punish trade-related producing sectors, and favors domestic consumers. Generally speaking, overvaluation is deflationary.

Undervaluation

Now suppose that Nation A undervalues the α by deliberately selling α's on the international currency market in order to obtain β's and γ's. The value of α in terms of β and γ will tend to fall as long as the government of A can systematically acquire foreign currency. Again suppose that the original exchange rate pattern was $1\,\alpha = 1\,\beta = 1\,\gamma$. Sales of α's by Nation A's government might drive the exchange value of α down to perhaps $1\,\alpha = 0.8\,\beta = 0.8\,\gamma$.

The international market effects of this undervaluation are similar to the devaluation effects depicted as $ED^0(R)$ shifts to $ED^1(R)$ in Fig. 15.3 and from $ES^0(R)$ to $ES^1(R)$ in Fig. 15.5. From the exporter's point of view (Fig. 15.3), undervaluation appears as an increase in the foreign demand function, resulting in more exports and higher α prices. It is like an export subsidy paid by the A government. From the importer's point of view (Fig. 15.5), undervaluation causes a decrease in the foreign supply function, reducing import volume and boosting domestic prices of import goods. It is like an import tax or tariff levied by Nation A on itself.

By encouraging exports and discouraging imports, undervaluation raises domestic prices, promotes economic activity in trade-related sectors, and is unfavorable to domestic consumers. Generally speaking, undervaluation is inflationary.

MULTIPLE EXCHANGE RATES

Alterations in national currency exchange rates, even if deliberate, are not usually thought of as trade policy in the same way as traditional import tariffs or export subsidies. However, there is one class of exchange-rate manipulation that can be viewed as trade policy in a more narrow or specific sense—multiple exchange rates.

Multiple exchange rates are often used by developing nations to stimulate or inhibit trade for specifically designated commodity groups. The central idea is that the official or authorized exchange rate between foreign and domestic currency depends, at least partly, on the product being traded. For instance, one exchange rate might apply for imports of television sets. Another rate might apply for imports of industrial drill presses. Differing rates also might apply for exports of diamonds versus exports of coffee.

To institute and sustain a multiple exchange-rate system, the national government must be able to control strictly the access to foreign currency by would-be domestic importers and access to local currency by exporters who earn foreign currencies from sales abroad. In addition, the government also must be able to document and monitor actual physical purchases and sales on the international market to ensure compliance with its multiple exchange-rate scheme.

In a multiple exchange-rate regime, the rate is deliberately undervalued for purchases of import items the government wishes to discourage or for sales of export items it wishes to encourage. The rate is deliberately overvalued for imports the government wishes to encourage or exports it wishes to discourage. Numerous rates may be adopted across broad or narrow product categories depending on the complexity of the scheme and the trade policy goals sought by the government. Consider a specific, relatively simple hypothetical example.

The nation of Fiberia has a large, traditional cotton- and textile-producing sector it wishes to protect and encourage. It also has a fledgling automobile manufacturing industry it wishes to promote. Since Fiberia is a relatively poor nation, the government also wants to keep domestic food prices as low as possible. One way Fiberia has chosen to pursue these goals is through a multiple exchange rate system operated by the Fiberian Central Bank (FCB), which has direct control of all foreign-exchange transactions.

For illustration, consider two import goods and two export goods purchased and sold by Fiberian merchants. The import goods are passenger cars and farm tractors. The two relevant export goods are cotton textiles and wheat. The initial equilibrium, across-the-board exchange rate between U.S. dollars and the Fiberian currency (denoted by ϕ) is 1 to 1. That is, $\$1.00 = \phi 1.00$.

The FCB managers of the multiple-exchange rate scheme now set two rates for exchanging ϕ's into dollars for potential imports. The reciprocals of these two rates are employed for exchanging dollars into ϕ's for potential exports. One rate is "overvalued" at $\phi 1.00 = \$1.10$ (or $\$1.00 = \phi 0.91$) and one rate is "undervalued" at $\phi 1.00 = \$0.90$ (or $\$1.00 = \phi 1.11$). On the import side, purchasers of foreign tractors get the overvalued rate but purchasers of foreign cars face the undervalued rate. Imagine for simplicity that on the international market, farm tractors and passenger cars cost $\$10,000$ each. So instead of costing $\phi 10,000$ each, tractors and passenger cars carry different prices inside Fiberia even though their international prices remain at $\$10,000$ each. Tractors now cost $\phi 9,091$ and imported cars cost $\phi 11,111$. So compared with the original, across-the-board exchange-rate regime, tractor imports are encouraged and passenger car imports are discouraged.

The export side reflects essentially the reverse situation. Sellers of textiles get an undervalued rate but wheat exporters face an overvalued rate. So textile exports that earn $\$10,000$ in foreign markets will now generate $\phi 11,111$ domestically rather than the original $\phi 10,000$. On the other hand, wheat exports earning $\$10,000$ on the world market will now return $\phi 9,091$ instead of $\phi 10,000$. Thus, textile exports are encouraged and wheat exports are discouraged with this multiple exchange-rate scheme.

As long as the FCB can maintain tight control on foreign currency transactions involving ϕ's, and as long as the Fiberian government can monitor and regulate compliance with the authorized international transactions, this multiple-rate program will tend to promote the cotton/textile sectors, protect the domestic automobile industry, and push down domestic food prices without involving large direct government outlays. It will, however, punish Fiberian wheat farmers with lower prices received and Fiberian purchasers of automobiles with higher prices paid.

SUMMARY

Exchange rates between national currencies are the prices of one country's currency in terms of other currencies. They translate domestic prices of goods, services, and other economic values across international borders. Like other prices, they are subject to change. Where currencies are freely traded on international money markets or when central authorities attempt to value their currency to balance international accounts, exchange rates move in accordance with differential effects of inflation, productivity, interest rates, and other macroeconomic forces among nations.

Since exchange-rate changes usually affect international transactions across the board, their movements can override and obscure the effects of other, more specific or narrow trade and economic policies. When a nation's currency rises in value relative to those of other countries, exports of goods and services tend to fall and imports tend to rise. When a nation's currency falls in relative value, exports tend to be stimulated and imports curtailed.

When a currency's value is rising internationally, domestic prices of traded goods tend to fall and foreign prices of the same goods tend to rise. When a currency's value is falling, domestic prices of traded goods tend to rise while international prices tend to fall. A rising exchange rate (appreciation) is deflationary, but a falling exchange rate (devaluation) is inflationary.

Higher-than-equilibrium exchange rates act like export taxes and import subsidies. Lower-than-equilibrium rates act like export subsidies and import tariffs. Therefore, some nations impose multiple exchange rates on their own currency relative to other monies. In such cases, differing rates apply to international transactions depending on the product or service being traded. Multiple exchange rates can be used to achieve results similar to tariffs, import quotas, export taxes, and export subsidies.

QUESTIONS

15.1 Assume that Nation A is an exporter of soybeans. Nation C also exports soybeans. Both sell to Nation B. After a period of relative stability in exchange rates, the γ of Nation C is devalued relative to the α of A and the β of B. Illustrate and discuss the implications of this change on the international soybean market, considering prices, production, consumption, and trade.

15.2 What kind of exchange-rate changes on the part of Nation B could change Nation A from an exporter of soybeans to an importer?

15.3 During a speech, an international trade expert asserts that her country's currency is "overvalued" relative to those of major trading partners. She also argues that this condition has the effect of an export tax on coffee exports from her country. Explain and illustrate.

15.4 The country of Trombonia employs a complex multiple exchange-rate system. The nation's central bank will exchange horns (the domestic currency) for international monies at various rates depending on the item to be sold or purchased. Here are a few examples from the Trombonia exchange rate schedule for horns and U.S. dollars.
   a For beef exports: 4 horns per dollar
   b For grain imports: 28 cents per horn
   c For incoming tourists: 5 horns per dollar
   d For packaged food imports: 20 cents per horn
   e For television exports: 4.3 horns per dollar
   f For traveling Trombonians: 21 cents per horn
   Discuss the trade policy aspects of these data from the Trombonian perspective.

ADDITIONAL READINGS

Caves, R. E., and Jones, R. W. 1981. *World Trade and Payments: An Introduction*, 3rd ed., Little, Brown and Co., Boston, Massachusetts, Chap. 18. (A mainly general equilibrium approach to currency devaluation and appreciation economics.)

Corden, W. M. 1971. *The Theory of Protection*, Clarendon Press, Oxford, England, pp. 87–92. (A good summary of protection via multiple exchange rates.)

Grennes, T. 1984. *International Economics*, Prentice-Hall, Englewood Cliffs, New Jersey, Chap. 15. (A general discussion of exchange rates, their effects and markets.)

Lindert, P. H., and Kindleberger, C. P. 1982. *International Economics*, 7th ed., Richard D. Irwin, Homewood, Illinois, Chap. 15. (This chapter on exchange rates features a discussion of the effects of devaluation and appreciation in the excess demand and supply framework.)

Longmire, J., and Morey, A. 1983. Strong Dollar Dampens Demand for U.S. Farm Exports, Foreign Agricultural Economic Report No. 193, Economic Research Service, U.S. Department of Agriculture, Washington, D.C. (December 1983). (An empirical study based on partial equilibrium analysis similar to that presented in this chapter.)

Walter, I. 1975. *International Economics*, Ronald Press, New York, New York, pp. 431–433. (A short discussion of multiple exchange rates.)

Chapter 16

Producer Protection, World Prices, and Trade Stability

Virtually everything in the previous 15 chapters of this book has emphasized the basic economics of various *national* trade policy schemes. Individual countries adopting these various schemes were assumed to face an aggregate, external international market. The shape and economic behavior of the "world" market have been largely outside our scope. However, in this final chapter, we take a brief look at how agricultural trade policy decisions of individual nations, both importers and exporters, can affect the level of international prices and their stability.

Our view will be rather circumscribed because we will use only the basic analytical tools and ideas that were developed previously. Our main objective will be to assess the systematic way in which trade policies, especially those designed to protect domestic *producers*, impinge on the world market. By implication, we will consider how these policies affect world market participants who do not or cannot provide economic protection to their own agricultural producers. We will capture a glimpse, in partial equilibrium terms, of how various national trade policies push an international market away from free trade results. Then we will assert some limited generalizations about these effects.

For instance, suppose we are interested in the world wheat market. Without going into specifics, we can assert that many wheat importers operate trade policy schemes designed to protect their domestic wheat producers. These include quotas, variable levies, deficiency payment or production subsidy programs, and mixing regulations. Several wheat exporters provide producer protection through export subsidies, market and price discrimination schemes, deficiency payments, and various other production subsidies. In addition, there is a fringe of small wheat importers and exporters who are more or less free traders on the world market, operating without much direct government intervention in their wheat trade or pricing.

Looking at this particular market, we might wish to know if and how the protectionist behavior of intervening importers and exporters alters the operation of the world wheat market for all participants, especially for the nonintervening fringe. Our analytical tools of demand and supply cannot answer all questions on this topic, but they can carry us at least part of the way toward a general appreciation of the forces at work.

THE ANALYTICAL SETTING

To explore how protective trade policy decisions by individual nations might affect international markets we need first to visualize a situation that is free of intervention. Consider the international market for a widely traded agricultural product q. In Fig. 16.1, the function DW is the horizontal sum of all free-market excess demand functions for q displayed by importing countries. Assume first that none of these importing nations is intervening directly in the markets or pricing of q. Similarly, SW is the horizontal summation of all free-market excess supply functions for q displayed by exporting countries. Assume that no policy intervention by export nation governments is occurring along SW.

In this context, DW can be called a world demand function for q and SW can be called a world supply function. The free-market world price would be p_1 and the quantity moving in trade would be q_1. We will suppose for this discussion that there are numerous countries involved on both sides of this international market. Naturally, we can expect that shifts in DW and SW will occur over time, causing p_1 and q_1 to alter. But as long as these two functions remain free of systematic intervention, the resulting prices and trade volumes on the world market will reflect free trade.

Now suppose that several importing nations institute protective policies on behalf of their own domestic producers of q. These policies could be tariffs, quotas, deficiency payments, variable levies, production subsidies, overvalued currency, and the like. With no exceptions, all of these protective measures will shift individual excess demand curves to the left and downward.

As the analyses of Chaps. 5, 6, 7, and 8 illustrate, a decrease in international demand is a pervasive result of protective trade policies on behalf of the domestic producing industry. Domestic producers expand output behind protective policies, supplanting imports in their own national markets. As individual nations' excess-demand curves move leftward, the world-demand curve function will fall to perhaps DW^*. With no change occurring in world supply

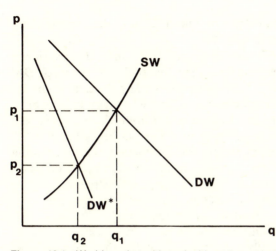

Figure 16.1 World market with and without importer intervention

conditions, reflected in *SW,* international prices will fall to p_2 and trade volume will dwindle to q_2. Hence, the general effect of producer protection by import nations is to place downward pressure on both world prices and trade volume.

Now imagine for a moment that the only departures from free trade are pursued by some of the exporting nations (Fig. 16.2). Consider *SW* as the free-trade aggregate of exporters' excess supply functions. Further, suppose that the policy interventions by export governments involve protection of domestic producers by means of export subsidies, production subsidies, market discrimination, undervalued currency, and the like. As the analyses of Chaps. 10 and 11 illustrate, protection of domestic producers shifts an individual nation's excess supply function to the right and downward. This occurs because domestic producers are encouraged to increase output beyond the volume associated with free trade. The aggregate impact on the world supply function is a shift from *SW* to perhaps *SW**. If *DW* holds steady, the net effect of protective trade policies by exporters is to put downward pressure on world prices from p_1 to p_2. However, there is clear upward pressure on trade volumes as export nations seek to push expanded output onto international markets (q_1 to q_2 in Fig. 16.2).

Now let us put the two previous scenarios together in Fig. 16.3. The protecting exporters are attempting to place their increased output of q onto the world market, but the protecting importers are stifling imports in order to reserve their domestic market for expanding domestic output. The result is a mutually reinforcing downward pressure on world prices, from p_1 to p_2 in Fig. 16.3. The net effect on trade volume at any time is uncertain, depending on whether the demand shrinkage or the supply expansion is the more powerful force. In Fig. 16.3, they are shown to be equal. This depiction is simply for convenience;

it could be either way. However, there is no question about the negative price effects of joint producer protection.

Note that in Figs. 16.1, 16.2, and 16.3, both *DW** and *SW** are shown to be steeper or more price inelastic than their free trade counterparts, *DW* and *SW*. This is not an accident. Most protective trade policies alter the individual nation's excess demand or excess supply curve so that it is more price insensitive (or inelastic) than the free trade function from which it is derived. On the import side, this tendency holds true for fixed tariffs, all manner of quotas, variable levies, deficiency payments, and production subsidies. On the export side, supply inelasticity is accentuated by export subsidies, production subsidies, and various market discrimination schemes. Virtually no protective scheme on behalf of domestic producers increases the international price responsiveness of a nation's excess demand or supply function.

When a demand or supply function becomes more price inelastic, the product in question exhibits potentially more price instability than previously. If additional price inelasticity is introduced into a demand function, any given fluctuations in the corresponding supply function will set off wider price swings than previously. The same is also true for given demand shifts against an increasingly inelastic supply function. Hence, producer protection by trading nations (1) presses international prices down as world market demand shifts to the left and world market supply shifts to the right from the free trade position and (2) enhances the potential for international price instability by increasing the inelasticity in both demand and supply functions.

In other words, by partially or entirely disconnecting domestic prices from world markets to protect local producers, governments contribute to downward pressure on international prices and to increased period-to-period fluctuation in those prices. Average world trade volume might increase or decrease compared with free trade. If domestic protection offered by importers is stronger

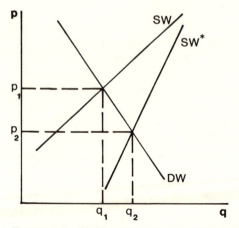

Figure 16.2 World market with and without exporter intervention

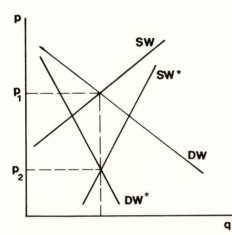

Figure 16.3 World market with importer and exporter intervention

than that offered by exporters, trade volume will be less than under free trade. If the reverse is true, trade volume will be larger.

AN ILLUSTRATIVE EXAMPLE OF PRICE EFFECTS AND STABILITY

Here is a specific, but plausible example that illustrates the main points advanced in the previous section. Assume that the unfettered free trade demand for product q fluctuates from year to year but remains within the bounds indicated by DW_1 and DW_2 in Fig. 16.4. Similarly, the unfettered free trade supply function fluctuates within the bounds indicated by SW_1 and SW_2. In this case, all free trade equilibrium price and quantity points from period to period will lie inside the shaded area A. Prices have the potential to fluctuate between 15 and 20 cents per pound, and traded quantities can fluctuate between 7.5 and 12.5 million tons. This is the free trade benchmark against which we will compare the effects of producer protection.

Now imagine that producer protection occurs on both sides of this market—some major importers and some major exporters are involved. On the demand side, DW_1^* and DW_2^* are the policy-burdened counterparts of DW_1 and DW_2 respectively. Similarly, SW_1^* and SW_2^* are the policy-burdened counterparts of SW_1 and SW_2 respectively. Note that in this illustration the *horizontal* fluctuation potential of both DW^* and SW^* is held to be the same as with free trade and the same in relation to each other. That is, the environmental or other forces at work in random or uncertain ways are the same whether or not free trade prevails. And for this example they are the same on both the demand and supply sides of the market.

Also note that DW^* and SW^* are steeper or more price inelastic than their free trade counterparts. In fact, they are each drawn to be twice as steep. This increase in price inelasticity results from the insulation of at least some

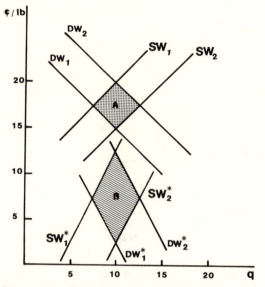

Figure 16.4 World demand and supply functions with and without producer protection

importers' and some exporters' domestic markets from world market vagaries. In this example, the policy-burdened market prices and quantities from period to period will lie inside the shaded area *B*.

Because the horizontal fluctuations of the various functions are constant, the potential quantity fluctuations with and without intervention are the same—between 7.5 and 12.5 million tons. (It need not have been so in general.) However, within area *B*, the zone of potential price fluctuation is wider and centered on a lower midpoint. In fact, policy-burdened price fluctuations in this example extend between 2.5 and 12.5 cents per pound, a range twice as wide as with free trade. The vertical elongation of area *B* compared with area *A* results from the increased inelasticity of *DW** and *SW** compared with *DW* and *SW*.

To press this illustrative example a little further, a modest numerical experiment was conducted to show how the specific changes in supply and demand shown here as the results of protective policy might actually impinge on world prices for *q*. First, the exact algebraic formulas for DW_1 and SW_1 were written down and solved for the equilibrium price (17.5 cents per pound). Then, two series of 25 random numbers each were drawn. One series was applied to DW_1 to shift it around unpredictably between DW_1 and DW_2. The other series was applied to SW_2 to shift it randomly between SW_1 and SW_2. For each random joint supply and demand shift, the resulting equilibrium price was obtained. When each of the 25 solutions is viewed as an annual or monthly observation, made in sequence, the "time series" labeled A in Fig. 16.5 emerges. This series is simply an ordered, random set of observations drawn from inside area *A* of Fig. 16.4.

Next, the same two series of random numbers in the same order were applied to DW_1^* and SW_1^*. The price solutions for this series are plotted and labeled as B in Fig. 16.5. This "time series" is an ordered, random series of observations drawn from area B in Fig. 16.4, but it is linked closely to the first set from A.

Because the same random horizontal shifts were applied to each set of demand and supply functions, the period-to-period price movements are similar. However, the free-trade prices (A) fluctuate about an average of 17.5 cents per pound, while the policy-burdened prices (B) fluctuate about 7.5 cents per pound. Moreover, set B fluctuates much more widely than set A in response to the same sequence of external forces. In particular, the standard deviation of price series A is 1.5 cents, while that of series B is 3.0 cents. From one period to the next, the average fluctuation in price series A is 1.7 cents. For series B, it is 3.5 cents.

While this specific example does not provide conclusive proof, it demonstrates the reasoning behind the widely held notion that producer protection by means of typical trade policy and related measures tends to lower world prices and make them more volatile.

FURTHER DESTABILIZING FACTORS

It also seems likely that national protective policies themselves may generate wider swings in world market supplies than otherwise would occur. These wider quantity fluctuations in turn create even stronger price gyrations than those associated with the equal horizontal shifts in excess demand and supply func-

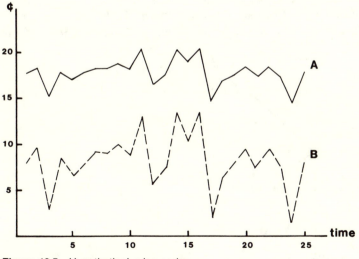

Figure 16.5 Hypothetical price series

tions postulated in the previous section. As intervening importers and exporters create more stable internal prices, unexpected shifts in domestic demand and supply conditions can create quantity surpluses or shortages that impinge directly on world markets. Because internal price adjustments are minimized, changes in quantities demanded or supplied domestically tend to be almost fully reflected on the world market. No internal price buffering effect occurs.

Consider now a rather simple analysis from a representative importer's point of view to illustrate this general line of reasoning. Nation A, a large importer of agricultural product q, faces a positively sloped excess supply function, $ES(R)$ in Fig. 16.6. Imagine that internal fluctuations in domestic supply and demand relations cause the free trade excess demand for Nation A to gyrate between ED_1 and ED_2. With no policy intervention, the country's imports would fluctuate between points indicated by f and g on the horizontal axis of Fig. 16.6. World prices and internal prices would be equal and move betwen b and c on the vertical axis.

Now assume that Nation A's government decides to keep its internal price stable at $\bar{p}$, midway between b and c. How this price stability is achieved is relatively unimportant here as long as sizable changes in government stocks are not involved. When excess demand is weak, as at ED_1, imports are curtailed administratively at e to protect $\bar{p}$ in the domestic market. This will push the world price down to a. Similarly, when excess demand is strong, as at ED_2, imports are encouraged up to h to hold the domestic price at $\bar{p}$. This might be done with import subsidies or by direct government purchases at the world price of d, with resale internally at $\bar{p}$.

By detaching its internal prices from the world market, Nation A contributes to larger international price and quantity swings than otherwise would transpire. Instead of fluctuating between f and g, the volume of Nation A's trade in this product will fluctuate between e and h. World prices, instead of moving between b and c, will gyrate between a and d as long as $ES(R)$ remains steady.

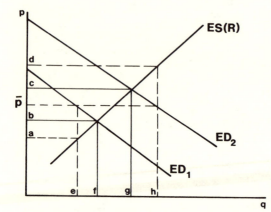

Figure 16.6 Trade effects of domestic price stabilization

The same conclusions emerge if a large exporter stabilizes and unhooks its internal price from fluctuations in the world market. In this case, the exporter might keep its internal prices stable by means of export subsidies when domestic excess supplies are large and by export controls when its internal supplies are tight. This behavior also will transfer internal market instability directly onto world markets without mitigation. Wider price and trade volume swings will occur than if internal and external market prices were more closely linked together.

SUMMARY

In this chapter we have shown by argument and illustration that protective trade policies pursued by individual countries on behalf of producers affect the behavior of the wider international market. Producer protection by importers and exporters puts clear downward pressure on world prices. In addition, the most widely employed trade policy schemes accentuate the price inelasticity of world demand and supply functions. This increased inelasticity creates the potential for wider period-to-period swings in world prices than otherwise would occur. Moreover, the tendency of prices to be more unstable in a policy-laden environment is further aggravated because producer protection by individual nations often detaches domestic prices from international prices, creating wider fluctuations in commodity imports and exports from trading nations than would occur with free trade.

QUESTIONS

16.1 Grainland is a very large exporter of corn to the world market. Its sales clearly influence world market prices. The government of Grainland acts to stabilize domestic prices of corn to both producers and users, but production is not directly controlled and large government inventories are not acquired or sold. Explain and illustrate why foreigners, both importers of corn and competitive foreign sellers, may be distressed by Grainland's action.

16.2 Until recently, the centrally planned country of Kremland followed a policy of virtual autarky in the production and consumption of feed grains. Expansion and contraction of livestock numbers closely paralleled the wide fluctuations in domestic grain output. Kremland's new policy is to hold livestock numbers relatively constant at recent high levels and supplement domestic feed supplies with imports without much regard for world prices. Discuss how this development would affect the world grain markets. Would it improve or worsen the situation described in question 1?

16.3 The small African republic of Rwongo purchases dry milk, butter, and other dairy products on the world market. There are very few dairy cows in this nation. The Rwongan government is quietly pleased when milk price guarantees are increased in Europe. Explain.

16.4 Assume that a partial return to free trade is negotiated internationally by nations importing and exporting sugar. Would you expect the volume of world trade in sugar to increase or decrease? Defend your reasoning. What would happen to world prices?

ADDITIONAL READINGS

Bale, M. D. and Lutz, E. 1979. The effects of trade intervention on international price instability, *Amer. Journal of Agricultural Economics*, 61:512-516. (Price stability with free trade is compared to that with tariffs, quotas, price fixing, variable levies, export controls, and autarky applied by importing and exporting nations using a simple algebraic system.)

Bigman, D. 1982. *Coping with Hunger: Toward a System of Food Security and Price Stabilization*, Ballinger Publishing Co., Cambridge, Massachusetts, Chaps. 6 and 7. (A relatively technical but interesting look at the price stabilizing aspects of free trade.)

Johnson, D. G. 1975. World agriculture, commodity policy, and price variability, *Amer. Journal of Agricultural Economics*, 57:823-828. (A nontechnical discussion.)

Josling, T. E. 1981. Domestic agricultural price policies and their interaction through trade, in: *Imperfect Markets in Agricultural Trade* (A. F. McCalla and T. E. Josling, eds.), Chap. 4, Allanheld Osmun, Montclair, New Jersey. (A partial equilibrium analysis using various trade policy schemes on either side of the international market.)

Index

Index